THIRD EDITION

JavaScript
Pocket Reference

David Flanagan

Beijing · Cambridge · Farnham · Köln · Sebastopol · Tokyo

JavaScript Pocket Reference, Third Edition
by David Flanagan

Copyright © 2012 David Flanagan. All rights reserved.
Printed in the United States of America.

Published by O'Reilly Media, Inc., 1005 Gravenstein Highway North, Sebastopol, CA 95472.

O'Reilly books may be purchased for educational, business, or sales promotional use. Online editions are also available for most titles (*http://my.safari booksonline.com*). For more information, contact our corporate/institutional sales department: (800) 998-9938 or *corporate@oreilly.com*.

Editor: Simon St. Laurent
Production Editor: Teresa Elsey
Proofreader: Kiel Van Horn
Indexer: Jay Marchand
Cover Designer: Karen Montgomery
Interior Designer: David Futato
Illustrator: Robert Romano

October 1998:	First Edition.
November 2002:	Second Edition.
April 2012:	Third Edition.

Revision History for the Third Edition:

2012-04-06	First release
2012-10-12	Second release
2013-04-19	Third release

See *http://oreilly.com/catalog/errata.csp?isbn=9781449316853* for release details.

ISBN: 978-1-449-31685-3

[LSI]

1366217005

Contents

Preface

JavaScript is the programming language of the Web. The overwhelming majority of modern websites use JavaScript, and all modern web browsers—on desktops, game consoles, tablets, and smartphones—include JavaScript interpreters, making JavaScript the most ubiquitous programming language in history. JavaScript is part of the triad of technologies that all Web developers must learn: HTML to specify the content of web pages, CSS to specify the presentation of those pages, and JavaScript to specify their behavior. Recently, with the advent of Node (*http://nodejs.org*), JavaScript has also become an important programming language for web servers.

This book is an excerpt from the more comprehensive *JavaScript: The Definitive Guide*. No material from the out-of-date second edition remains. I'm hopeful that some readers will find this shorter and denser book more useful than the larger and more intimidating volume from which it came. This pocket reference follows the same basic outline as the larger book: Chapters 1 through 9 cover the core JavaScript language, starting with fundamental matters of language syntax—types, values, variables, operators, statements—and moving on to coverage of JavaScript objects, arrays, functions and classes. These chapters cover the language itself, and are equally relevant to programmers who will use JavaScript in web browsers and programmers who will be using Node on the server-side.

To be useful, every language must have a platform or standard library of functions for performing things like basic input and output. The core JavaScript language defines a minimal API for working with text, arrays, dates, and regular expressions but does not include any input or output functionality. Input and output (as well as more sophisticated features, such as networking, storage, and graphics) are the responsibility of the "host environment" within which JavaScript is embedded. The most common host environment is a web browser. Chapters 1 through 9 cover the language's minimal built-in API. Chapters 10 through 14 cover the web browser host environment and explain how to use "client-side JavaScript" to create dynamic web pages and web applications.

The number of JavaScript APIs implemented by web browsers has grown explosively in recent years, and it is not possible to cover them all in a book of this size. Chapters 10 through 14 cover the most important and fundamental parts of client-side JavaScript: windows, documents, elements, styles, events, networking and storage. Once you master these, it is easy to pick up additional client-side APIs, which you can read about in *JavaScript: The Definitive Guide*. (Or in *Canvas Pocket Reference* and *jQuery Pocket Reference*, which are also excerpts from *The Definitive Guide*.)

Although the Node programming environment is becoming more and more important, there is simply not room in this pocket reference to include any information about server-side JavaScript. You can learn more at *http://nodejs.org*. Similarly, there is no room in the book for an API reference section. Again, I refer you to *JavaScript: The Definitive Guide*, or to online JavaScript references such as the excellent Mozilla Developer Network at *http://developer.mozilla.org/*.

The examples in this book can be downloaded from the book's web page, which will also include errata if any errors are discovered after publication:

http://shop.oreilly.com/product/0636920011460.do

In general, you may use the examples in this book in your programs and documentation. You do not need to contact us for permission unless you're reproducing a significant portion of the code. We appreciate, but do not require, an attribution like this: "From *JavaScript Pocket Reference*, third edition, by David Flanagan (O'Reilly). Copyright 2012 David Flanagan, 978-1-449-31685-3." If you feel your use of code examples falls outside fair use or the permission given here, feel free to contact us at *permissions@oreilly.com*.

To comment or ask technical questions about this book, send email to:

> *bookquestions@oreilly.com*

This book is also available from the Safari Books Online service. For full digital access to this book and others on similar topics from O'Reilly and other publishers, visit *http://www.sa faribooksonline.com/*.

I'd like to thank my editor, Simon St. Laurent, for challenging me to excerpt *The Definitive Guide* down to this more manageable size and also the O'Reilly production staff, who always manage to make my books look great.

CHAPTER 1

Lexical Structure

JavaScript programs are written using the Unicode character set. Unicode is a superset of ASCII and Latin-1 and supports virtually every written language currently used on the planet.

JavaScript is a case-sensitive language. This means that language keywords, variables, function names, and other *identifiers* must always be typed with a consistent capitalization of letters. The `while` keyword, for example, must be typed "while," not "While" or "WHILE." Similarly, `online`, `Online`, `OnLine`, and `ONLINE` are four distinct variable names.

Comments

JavaScript supports two styles of comments. Any text between a // and the end of a line is treated as a comment and is ignored by JavaScript. Any text between the characters /* and */ is also treated as a comment; these comments may span multiple lines but may not be nested. The following lines of code are all legal JavaScript comments:

```
// This is a single-line comment.
/* This is also a comment */  // And here is another.
/*
 * This is yet another comment.
 * It has multiple lines.
 */
```

Identifiers and Reserved Words

An *identifier* is simply a name. In JavaScript, identifiers are used to name variables and functions and to provide labels for certain loops in JavaScript code. A JavaScript identifier must begin with a letter, an underscore (_), or a dollar sign ($). Subsequent characters can be letters, digits, underscores, or dollar signs.

JavaScript reserves a number of identifiers as the keywords of the language itself. You cannot use these words as identifiers in your programs:

```
break      delete     function    return     typeof
case       do         if          switch     var
catch      else       in          this       void
continue   false      instanceof  throw      while
debugger   finally    new         true       with
default    for        null        try
```

JavaScript also reserves certain keywords that are not currently used by the language but which might be used in future versions. ECMAScript 5 reserves the following words:

```
class  const  enum  export  extends  import  super
```

In addition, the following words, which are legal in ordinary JavaScript code, are reserved in strict mode:

```
implements  let      private    public  yield
interface   package  protected  static
```

Strict mode also imposes restrictions on the use of the following identifiers. They are not fully reserved, but they are not allowed as variable, function, or parameter names:

```
arguments  eval
```

ECMAScript 3 reserved all the keywords of the Java language, and although this has been relaxed in ECMAScript 5, you should still avoid all of these identifiers if you plan to run your code under an ECMAScript 3 implementation of JavaScript:

```
abstract  double   goto        native     static
boolean   enum     implements  package    super
byte      export   import      private    synchronized
char      extends  int         protected  throws
```

---

class	final	interface	public	transient
const	float	long	short	volatile

Optional Semicolons

Like many programming languages, JavaScript uses the semicolon (;) to separate statements (see Chapter 4) from each other. This is important to make the meaning of your code clear: without a separator, the end of one statement might appear to be the beginning of the next, or vice versa. In JavaScript, you can usually omit the semicolon between two statements if those statements are written on separate lines. (You can also omit a semicolon at the end of a program or if the next token in the program is a closing curly brace }.) Many JavaScript programmers (and the code in this book) use semicolons to explicitly mark the ends of statements, even where they are not required. Another style is to omit semicolons whenever possible, using them only in the few situations that require them. Whichever style you choose, there are a few details you should understand about optional semicolons in JavaScript.

Consider the following code. Since the two statements appear on separate lines, the first semicolon could be omitted:

```
a = 3;
b = 4;
```

Written as follows, however, the first semicolon is required:

```
a = 3; b = 4;
```

Note that JavaScript does not treat every line break as a semicolon: it usually treats line breaks as semicolons only if it can't parse the code without the semicolons. More formally, JavaScript interprets a line break as a semicolon if it appears after the return, break, or continue keywords, or before the ++ or -- operators, or if the next nonspace character cannot be interpreted as a continuation of the current statement.

These statement termination rules lead to some surprising cases. This code looks like two separate statements separated with a newline:

```
var y = x + f
(a+b).toString()
```

But the parentheses on the second line of code can be interpreted as a function invocation of f from the first line, and JavaScript interprets the code like this:

```
var y = x + f(a+b).toString();
```

CHAPTER 2

Types, Values, and Variables

Computer programs work by manipulating *values*, such as the number 3.14 or the text "Hello World." The kinds of values that can be represented and manipulated in a programming language are known as *types*. When a program needs to retain a value for future use, it assigns the value to (or "stores" the value in) a *variable*. A variable defines a symbolic name for a value and allows the value to be referred to by name.

JavaScript types can be divided into two categories: *primitive types* and *object types*. JavaScript's primitive types include numbers, strings of text (known as *strings*), and Boolean truth values (known as *booleans*). The first few sections of this chapter explain JavaScript's primitive types. (Chapters 5, 6, and 7 describe three kinds of JavaScript object types.)

JavaScript converts values liberally from one type to another. If a program expects a string, for example, and you give it a number, it will automatically convert the number to a string for you. If you use a nonboolean value where a boolean is expected, JavaScript will convert accordingly. "Type Conversions" on page 15 describes JavaScript's type conversions.

JavaScript variables are *untyped*: you can assign a value of any type to a variable, and you can later assign a value of a different type to the same variable. Variables are *declared* with the var keyword. JavaScript uses *lexical scoping*. Variables declared outside of a function are *global variables* and are visible everywhere in a JavaScript program. Variables declared inside a function have *function scope* and are visible only to code that appears inside that function. "Variable Declaration" on page 19 covers variables in more detail.

Numbers

Unlike many languages, JavaScript does not make a distinction between integer values and floating-point values. All numbers in JavaScript are represented as floating-point values. JavaScript represents numbers using the 64-bit floating-point format defined by the IEEE 754 standard, which means it can represent numbers as large as $\pm 1.7976931348623157 \times 10^{308}$ and as small as $\pm 5 \times 10^{-324}$.

The JavaScript number format allows you to exactly represent all the integers between –9007199254740992 (-2^{53}) and 9007199254740992 (2^{53}), inclusive. If you use integer values larger than this, you may lose precision in the trailing digits. Note, however, that certain operations in JavaScript (such as array indexing and the bitwise operators described in Chapter 3) are performed with 32-bit integers.

When a number appears directly in a JavaScript program, it's called a *numeric literal*. JavaScript supports numeric literals in several formats. Note that any numeric literal can be preceded by a minus sign (-) to make the number negative.

In a JavaScript program, a base-10 integer is written as a sequence of digits. For example:

```
0
1024
```

In addition to base-10 integer literals, JavaScript recognizes hexadecimal (base-16) values. A hexadecimal literal begins with "0x" or "0X", followed by a string of hexadecimal digits. A hexadecimal digit is one of the digits 0 through 9 or the letters a (or A) through f (or F), which represent values 10 through 15. Here are examples of hexadecimal integer literals:

```
0xff  // 15*16 + 15 = 255 (base 10)
0xCAFE911
```

Floating-point literals can have a decimal point; they use the traditional syntax for real numbers. A real value is represented as the integral part of the number, followed by a decimal point and the fractional part of the number.

Floating-point literals may also be represented using exponential notation: a real number followed by the letter e (or E), followed by an optional plus or minus sign, followed by an integer exponent. This notation represents the real number multiplied by 10 to the power of the exponent.

More succinctly, the syntax is:

```
[digits][.digits][(E|e)[(+|-)]digits]
```

For example:

```
3.14
6.02e23       // 6.02 × 10²³
1.4738223E-32 // 1.4738223 × 10⁻³²
```

JavaScript programs work with numbers using the arithmetic operators that the language provides. These include + for addition, - for subtraction, * for multiplication, / for division, and % for modulo (remainder after division). Full details on these and other operators can be found in Chapter 3.

In addition to these basic arithmetic operators, JavaScript supports more complex mathematical operations through a set of functions and constants defined as properties of the Math object:

```
Math.pow(2,53)  // => 9007199254740992: 2 to the power 53
Math.round(.6)  // => 1.0: round to the nearest integer
Math.ceil(.6)   // => 1.0: round up to an integer
Math.floor(.6)  // => 0.0: round down to an integer
Math.abs(-5)    // => 5: absolute value
Math.max(x,y,z) // Return the largest argument
Math.min(x,y,z) // Return the smallest argument
Math.random()   // Pseudo-random number 0 <= x < 1.0
```

```
Math.PI          // π
Math.E           // e: The base of the natural logarithm
Math.sqrt(3)     // The square root of 3
Math.pow(3,1/3)  // The cube root of 3
Math.sin(0)      // Trig: also Math.cos, Math.atan, etc.
Math.log(10)     // Natural logarithm of 10
Math.log(100)/Math.LN10 // Base 10 logarithm of 100
Math.log(512)/Math.LN2  // Base 2 logarithm of 512
Math.exp(3)                 // Math.E cubed
```

Arithmetic in JavaScript does not raise errors in cases of over-flow, underflow, or division by zero. When the result of a numeric operation is larger than the largest representable number (overflow), the result is a special infinity value, which Java-Script prints as `Infinity`. Similarly, when a negative value becomes larger than the largest representable negative number, the result is negative infinity, printed as `-Infinity`. The infinite values behave as you would expect: adding, subtracting, multiplying, or dividing them by anything results in an infinite value (possibly with the sign reversed).

Division by zero is not an error in JavaScript: it simply returns infinity or negative infinity. There is one exception, however: zero divided by zero does not have a well-defined value, and the result of this operation is the special not-a-number value, printed as `NaN`. `NaN` also arises if you attempt to divide infinity by infinity, or take the square root of a negative number or use arithmetic operators with nonnumeric operands that cannot be converted to numbers.

JavaScript predefines global variables `Infinity` and `NaN` to hold the positive infinity and not-a-number value.

The not-a-number value has one unusual feature in JavaScript: it does not compare equal to any other value, including itself. This means that you can't write `x == NaN` to determine whether the value of a variable `x` is `NaN`. Instead, you should write `x != x`. That expression will be true if, and only if, `x` is `NaN`. The function `isNaN()` is similar. It returns `true` if its argument is `NaN`, or if that argument is a nonnumeric value such as a string or an object. The related function `isFinite()` returns `true` if its argument is a number other than `NaN`, `Infinity`, or `-Infinity`.

There are infinitely many real numbers, but only a finite number of them (18437736874454810627, to be exact) can be represented exactly by the JavaScript floating-point format. This means that when you're working with real numbers in JavaScript, the representation of the number will often be an approximation of the actual number and small rounding errors will occur.

Text

A *string* is an immutable ordered sequence of 16-bit values, each of which typically represents a Unicode character—strings are JavaScript's type for representing text. The *length* of a string is the number of 16-bit values it contains. JavaScript's strings (and its arrays) use zero-based indexing: the first 16-bit value is at position 0, the second at position 1 and so on. The *empty string* is the string of length 0. JavaScript does not have a special type that represents a single element of a string. To represent a single 16-bit value, simply use a string that has a length of 1.

String Literals

To include a string literally in a JavaScript program, simply enclose the characters of the string within a matched pair of single or double quotes (' or "). Double-quote characters may be contained within strings delimited by single-quote characters, and single-quote characters may be contained within strings delimited by double quotes. Here are examples of string literals:

```
""   // The empty string: it has zero characters
'name="myform"'
"Wouldn't you prefer O'Reilly's book?"
"This string\nhas two lines"
"π = 3.14"
```

The backslash character (\) has a special purpose in JavaScript strings. Combined with the character that follows it, it represents a character that is not otherwise representable within the string. For example, \n is an *escape sequence* that represents a newline character.

Another example is the \' escape, which represents the single quote (or apostrophe) character. This escape sequence is useful when you need to include an apostrophe in a string literal that is contained within single quotes. You can see why these are called escape sequences: the backslash allows you to escape from the usual interpretation of the single-quote character. Instead of using it to mark the end of the string, you use it as an apostrophe:

```
'You\'re right, it can\'t be a quote'
```

Table 2-1 lists the JavaScript escape sequences and the characters they represent. Two escape sequences are generic and can be used to represent any character by specifying its Latin-1 or Unicode character code as a hexadecimal number. For example, the sequence \xA9 represents the copyright symbol, which has the Latin-1 encoding given by the hexadecimal number A9. Similarly, the \u escape represents an arbitrary Unicode character specified by four hexadecimal digits; \u03c0 represents the character π, for example.

Table 2-1. JavaScript escape sequences

Sequence	Character represented
\0	The NUL character (\u0000)
\b	Backspace (\u0008)
\t	Horizontal tab (\u0009)
\n	Newline (\u000A)
\v	Vertical tab (\u000B)
\f	Form feed (\u000C)
\r	Carriage return (\u000D)
\"	Double quote (\u0022)
\'	Apostrophe or single quote (\u0027)
\\	Backslash (\u005C)

Sequence	Character represented
\x *XX*	The Latin-1 character specified by the two hexadecimal digits *XX*
\u *XXXX*	The Unicode character specified by the four hexadecimal digits *XXXX*

If the \ character precedes any character other than those shown in Table 2-1, the backslash is simply ignored (although future versions of the language may, of course, define new escape sequences). For example, \# is the same as #. ECMAScript 5 allows a backslash before a line break to break a string literal across multiple lines.

One of the built-in features of JavaScript is the ability to *concatenate* strings. If you use the + operator with numbers, it adds them. But if you use this operator on strings, it joins them by appending the second to the first. For example:

```
msg = "Hello, " + "world";   // => "Hello, world"
```

To determine the length of a string—the number of 16-bit values it contains—use the length property of the string. Determine the length of a string s like this:

```
s.length
```

In addition to this length property, there are a number of methods you can invoke on strings (as always, see the reference section for complete details):

```
var s = "hello, world" // Start with some text.
s.charAt(0)            // => "h": the first character.
s.charAt(s.length-1)   // => "d": the last character.
s.substring(1,4)       // => "ell": chars 2, 3, and 4
s.slice(1,4)           // => "ell": same thing
s.slice(-3)            // => "rld": last 3 characters
s.indexOf("l")         // => 2: position of first l.
s.lastIndexOf("l")     // => 10: position of last l.
s.indexOf("l", 3)      // => 3: position at or after 3
s.split(", ")          // => ["hello", "world"]
s.replace("h", "H")    // => "Hello, world":
                       //    replaces all instances
s.toUpperCase()        // => "HELLO, WORLD"
```

Remember that strings are immutable in JavaScript. Methods like `replace()` and `toUpperCase()` return new strings: they do not modify the string on which they are invoked.

In ECMAScript 5, strings can be treated like read-only arrays, and you can access individual characters (16-bit values) from a string using square brackets instead of the `charAt()` method:

```
s = "hello, world";
s[0]                   // => "h"
s[s.length-1]          // => "d"
```

Boolean Values

A boolean value represents truth or falsehood, on or off, yes or no. There are only two possible values of this type. The reserved words `true` and `false` evaluate to these two values.

Boolean values are generally the result of comparisons you make in your JavaScript programs. For example:

```
a == 4
```

This code tests to see whether the value of the variable `a` is equal to the number `4`. If it is, the result of this comparison is the boolean value `true`. If `a` is not equal to `4`, the result of the comparison is `false`.

Boolean values are commonly used in JavaScript control structures. For example, the `if/else` statement in JavaScript performs one action if a boolean value is `true` and another action if the value is `false`. You usually combine a comparison that creates a boolean value directly with a statement that uses it. The result looks like this:

```
if (a == 4)
  b = b + 1;
else
  a = a + 1;
```

This code checks whether `a` equals `4`. If so, it adds `1` to `b`; otherwise, it adds `1` to `a`.

As we'll discuss in "Type Conversions" on page 15, any Java-Script value can be converted to a boolean value. The following values convert to, and therefore work like, `false`:

```
undefined
null
0
-0
NaN
""   // the empty string
```

All other values, including all objects (and arrays) convert to, and work like, `true`. `false`, and the six values that convert to it, are sometimes called *falsy* values, and all other values are called *truthy*. Any time JavaScript expects a boolean value, a falsy value works like `false` and a truthy value works like `true`.

As an example, suppose that the variable o either holds an object or the value `null`. You can test explicitly to see if o is non-null with an `if` statement like this:

```
if (o !== null) ...
```

The not-equal operator `!==` compares o to `null` and evaluates to either `true` or `false`. But you can omit the comparison and instead rely on the fact that `null` is falsy and objects are truthy:

```
if (o) ...
```

In the first case, the body of the `if` will be executed only if o is not `null`. The second case is less strict: it will execute the body of the `if` only if o is not `false` or any falsy value (such as `null` or `undefined`). Which `if` statement is appropriate for your program really depends on what values you expect to be assigned to o. If you need to distinguish `null` from `0` and `""`, then you should use an explicit comparison.

null and undefined

`null` is a language keyword that evaluates to a special value that is usually used to indicate the absence of a value. Using the `typeof` operator on `null` returns the string "object," indicating that `null` can be thought of as a special object value that

indicates "no object." In practice, however, null is typically
regarded as the sole member of its own type, and it can be used
to indicate "no value" for numbers and strings as well as objects. Most programming languages have an equivalent to Java-
Script's null: you may be familiar with it as null or nil.

JavaScript also has a second value that indicates absence of
value. The undefined value represents a deeper kind of absence. It is the value of variables that have not been initialized
and the value you get when you query the value of an object
property or array element that does not exist. The undefined
value is also returned by functions that have no return value,
and the value of function parameters for which no argument is
supplied. undefined is a predefined global variable (not a language keyword like null) that is initialized to the undefined
value. If you apply the typeof operator to the undefined value,
it returns "undefined," indicating that this value is the sole
member of a special type.

Despite these differences, null and undefined both indicate an
absence of value and can often be used interchangeably. The
equality operator == considers them to be equal. (Use the strict
equality operator === to distinguish them.) Both are falsy
values—they behave like false when a boolean value is required. Neither null nor undefined have any properties or
methods. In fact, using . or [] to access a property or method
of these values causes a TypeError.

The Global Object

The sections above have explained JavaScript's primitive types
and values. Object types—objects, arrays, and functions—are
covered in chapters of their own later in this book. But there is
one very important object value that we must cover now. The
global object is a regular JavaScript object that serves a very
important purpose: the properties of this object are the globally
defined symbols that are available to a JavaScript program.
When the JavaScript interpreter starts (or whenever a web

browser loads a new page), it creates a new global object and gives it an initial set of properties that define:

- Global properties like undefined, Infinity, and NaN
- Global functions like isNaN(), parseInt() ("Type Conversions" on page 15), and eval() ("Evaluation Expressions" on page 43).
- Constructor functions like Date(), RegExp(), String(), Object(), and Array()
- Global objects like Math and JSON ("Serializing Properties and Objects" on page 84)

The initial properties of the global object are not reserved words, but they deserve to be treated as if they are. This chapter has already described some of these global properties. Most of the others will be covered elsewhere in this book.

In top-level code—JavaScript code that is not part of a function—you can use the JavaScript keyword this to refer to the global object:

```
var global = this; // /refer to the global object
```

In client-side JavaScript, the Window object serves as the global object. This global Window object has a self-referential window property that can be used to refer to the global object. The Window object defines the core global properties, but it also defines quite a few other globals that are specific to web browsers and client-side JavaScript (see Chapter 10).

When first created, the global object defines all of JavaScript's predefined global values. But this special object also holds program-defined globals as well. If your code declares a global variable, that variable is a property of the global object.

Type Conversions

JavaScript is very flexible about the types of values it requires. We've seen this for booleans: when JavaScript expects a boolean value, you may supply a value of any type, and

JavaScript will convert it as needed. Some values ("truthy" values) convert to **true** and others ("falsy" values) convert to **false**. The same is true for other types: if JavaScript wants a string, it will convert whatever value you give it to a string. If JavaScript wants a number, it will try to convert the value you give it to a number (or to **NaN** if it cannot perform a meaningful conversion). Some examples:

```
10 + " objects"   // => "10 objects". 10 -> string
"7" * "4"         // => 28: both strings -> numbers
var n = 1 - "x";  // => NaN: "x" can't convert to a number
n + " objects"    // => "NaN objects": NaN -> "NaN"
```

Table 2-2 summarizes how values convert from one type to another in JavaScript. Bold entries in the table highlight conversions that you may find surprising. Empty cells indicate that no conversion is necessary and none is performed.

Table 2-2. JavaScript type conversions

Value	Converted to:			
	String	**Number**	**Boolean**	**Object**
undefined	"undefined"	NaN	false	*throws TypeError*
null	"null"	0	false	*throws TypeError*
true	"true"	**1**		Boolean(true)
false	"false"	0		Boolean(false)
"" (empty string)		0	**false**	String("")
"1.2" (non-empty, numeric)		1.2	true	String("1.2")
"one" (non-empty, non-numeric)		NaN	true	String("one")
0	"0"		**false**	Number(0)
-0	"0"		**false**	Number(-0)
NaN	"NaN"		**false**	Number(NaN)
Infinity	"Infinity"		true	Number(Infinity)

Value	Converted to:			
	String	Number	Boolean	Object
-Infinity	"-Infinity"		true	Number(-Infinity)
1 (finite, non-zero)	"1"		true	Number(1)
{} (any object)	toString()	toString() or valueOf()	true	
[] (empty array)	""	0	true	
[9] (1 numeric elt)	"9"	9	true	
['a'] (any other array)	*use join() method*	NaN	true	
function() {} (any function)	*function source*	NaN	true	

Because JavaScript can convert values flexibly, its == equality operator is also flexible with its notion of equality. All of the following comparisons are true, for example:

```
null == undefined // These two are treated as equal.
"0" == 0          // String -> a number before comparing.
0 == false        // Boolean -> number before comparing.
"0" == false      // Both operands -> 0 before comparing.
```

Although JavaScript performs many type conversions automatically, you may sometimes need to perform an explicit conversion, or you may prefer to make the conversions explicit to keep your code clearer.

The simplest way to perform an explicit type conversion is to use the Boolean(), Number(), String(), or Object() functions:

```
Number("3")     // => 3
String(false)   // => "false" Or false.toString()
Boolean([])     // => true
Object(3)       // => new Number(3)
```

Note that any value other than `null` or `undefined` has a `toString()` method and the result of this method is usually the same as that returned by the `String()` function.

Certain JavaScript operators perform implicit type conversions, and are sometimes used for the purposes of type conversion. If one operand of the + operator is a string, it converts the other one to a string. The unary + operator converts its operand to a number. And the unary ! operator converts its operand to a boolean and negates it. These facts lead to the following type conversion idioms that you may see in some code:

```
x + "" // Same as String(x)
+x     // Same as Number(x). Also x-0
!!x    // Same as Boolean(x). Note double !
```

Formatting and parsing numbers are common tasks in computer programs and JavaScript has specialized functions and methods that provide more precise control over number-to-string and string-to-number conversions.

The `toString()` method defined by the Number class accepts an optional argument that specifies a radix, or base, for the conversion. If you do not specify the argument, the conversion is done in base 10. However, you can also convert numbers in other bases (between 2 and 36). For example:

```
var n = 17;
binary_string = n.toString(2);       // Evaluates to "10001"
octal_string = "0" + n.toString(8);  // Evaluates to "021"
hex_string = "0x" + n.toString(16);  // Evaluates to "0x11"
```

When working with financial or scientific data, you may want to convert numbers to strings in ways that give you control over the number of decimal places or the number of significant digits in the output, or you may want to control whether exponential notation is used. The Number class defines three methods for these kinds of number-to-string conversions:

```
var n = 123456.789;
n.toFixed(2);        // "123456.79"
n.toExponential(3);  // "1.235e+5"
n.toPrecision(7);    // "123456.8"
```

If you pass a string to the `Number()` conversion function, it attempts to parse that string as an integer or floating-point literal. That function only works for base-10 integers, and does not allow trailing characters that are not part of the literal. The `parseInt()` and `parseFloat()` functions (these are global functions, not methods of any class) are more flexible. `parseInt()` parses only integers, while `parseFloat()` parses both integers and floating-point numbers. If a string begins with "0x" or "0X," `parseInt()` interprets it as a hexadecimal number. Both `parseInt()` and `parseFloat()` skip leading whitespace, parse as many numeric characters as they can, and ignore anything that follows. If the first nonspace character is not part of a valid numeric literal, they return `NaN`:

```
parseInt("3 blind mice")     // => 3
parseFloat(" 3.14 meters")   // => 3.14
parseInt("-12.34")           // => -12
parseInt("0xFF")             // => 255
parseFloat("$72.47");        // => NaN
```

`parseInt()` accepts an optional second argument specifying the radix (base) of the number to be parsed. Legal values are between 2 and 36. For example:

```
parseInt("11", 2);           // => 3 (1*2 + 1)
parseInt("077", 8);          // => 63 (7*8 + 7)
parseInt("ff", 16);          // => 255 (15*16 + 15)
```

Variable Declaration

Before you use a variable in a JavaScript program, you should *declare* it. Variables are declared with the **var** keyword, like this:

```
var i;
var sum;
```

You can also declare multiple variables with the same **var** keyword:

```
var i, sum;
```

And you can combine variable declaration with variable initialization:

```
var message = "hello";
var i = 0, j = 0, k = 0;
```

If you don't specify an initial value for a variable with the **var** statement, the variable is declared, but its value is **undefined** until your code stores a value into it.

Note that the **var** statement can also appear as part of the **for** and **for/in** loops (introduced in Chapter 4), allowing you to succinctly declare the loop variable as part of the loop syntax itself. For example:

```
for(var i = 0; i < 10; i++) console.log(i);
for(var i = 0, j=10; i < 10; i++,j--) console.log(i*j);
for(var p in o) console.log(p);
```

If you're used to statically typed languages such as C or Java, you will have noticed that there is no type associated with JavaScript's variable declarations. A JavaScript variable can hold a value of any type. For example, it is perfectly legal in JavaScript to assign a number to a variable and then later assign a string to that variable:

```
var i = 10;
i = "ten";
```

It is legal and harmless to declare a variable more than once with the **var** statement. If the repeated declaration has an initializer, it acts as if it were simply an assignment statement.

If you attempt to read the value of an undeclared variable, JavaScript generates an error. In ECMAScript 5 strict mode (see "use strict" in Chapter 4), it is also an error to assign a value to an undeclared variable. Historically, however, and in nonstrict mode, if you assign a value to an undeclared variable, Java-Script actually creates that variable as a property of the global object, and it works much like a properly declared global variable. This means that you can get away with leaving your global variables undeclared. This is a bad habit and a source of bugs, however, and you should always declare your variables with **var**.

The *scope* of a variable is the region of your program source code in which it is defined. A *global* variable has global scope; it is defined everywhere in your JavaScript code. On the other hand, variables declared within a function are defined only within the body of the function. They are *local* variables and have local scope. Function parameters also count as local variables and are defined only within the body of the function.

Within the body of a function, a local variable takes precedence over a global variable with the same name. Although you can get away with not using the **var** statement when you write code in the global scope, you must always use **var** to declare local variables. Function definitions can be nested. Each function has its own local scope, so it is possible to have several nested layers of local scope.

In some C-like programming languages, each block of code within curly braces has its own scope, and variables are not visible outside of the block in which they are declared. This is called *block scope*, and JavaScript does *not* have it. Instead, JavaScript uses *function scope*: variables are visible within the function in which they are defined and within any functions that are nested within that function.

JavaScript's function scope means that all variables declared within a function are visible *throughout* the body of the function. Curiously, this means that variables are even visible before they are declared. This feature of JavaScript is informally known as *hoisting*: JavaScript code behaves as if all variable declarations in a function (but not any associated assignments) are "hoisted" to the top of the function.

CHAPTER 3

Expressions and Operators

An *expression* is a phrase of JavaScript that a JavaScript interpreter can *evaluate* to produce a value. A constant embedded literally in your program is a very simple kind of expression. A variable name is also a simple expression that evaluates to whatever value has been assigned to that variable. Complex expressions are built from simpler expressions. An array access expression, for example, consists of one expression that evaluates to an array followed by an open square bracket, an expression that evaluates to an integer, and a close square bracket. This new, more complex expression evaluates to the value stored at the specified index of the specified array. Similarly, a function invocation expression consists of one expression that evaluates to a function object and zero or more additional expressions that are used as the arguments to the function.

The most common way to build a complex expression out of simpler expressions is with an *operator*. An operator combines the values of its *operands* (usually two of them) in some way and evaluates to a new value. The multiplication operator * is a simple example. The expression x * y evaluates to the product of the values of the expressions x and y. For simplicity, we sometimes say that an operator *returns* a value rather than "evaluates to" a value.

Expressions

The simplest expressions, known as *primary expressions*, are those that stand alone—they do not include any simpler expressions. Primary expressions in JavaScript are constant or *literal* values, certain language keywords, and variable references.

Literals are constant values that are embedded directly in your program. They look like these:

```
1.23       // A number literal
"hello"    // A string literal
/pattern/  // A regular expression literal
```

Reserved words like `true`, `false`, `null`, and `this` are primary expressions.

Finally, the third type of primary expression is the bare variable reference:

```
i      // Evaluates to the value of the variable i.
sum    // Evaluates to the value of the variable sum.
```

When any identifier appears by itself in a program, JavaScript assumes it is a variable and looks up its value. If no variable with that name exists, the expression evaluates to the `undefined` value. In the strict mode of ECMAScript 5, however, an attempt to evaluate a nonexistent variable throws a ReferenceError instead.

Initializers

Object and array *initializers* are expressions whose value is a newly created object or array. These initializer expressions are sometimes called "object literals" and "array literals." Unlike true literals, however, they are not primary expressions, because they include a number of subexpressions that specify property and element values.

An array initializer is a comma-separated list of expressions contained within square brackets. The value of an array initializer is a newly created array. The elements of this new array are initialized to the values of the comma-separated expressions:

```
[]          // An empty array
[1+2,3+4] // A 2-element array with elts 3 and 7.
```

The element expressions in an array initializer can themselves be array initializers, which means that these expressions can create nested arrays:

```
var matrix = [[1,2,3], [4,5,6], [7,8,9]];
```

A single trailing comma is allowed after the last expression in an array initializer.

Object initializer expressions are like array initializer expressions, but the square brackets are replaced by curly braces, and each subexpression is prefixed with a property name and a colon:

```
var p = { x:2, y:1 }; // An object with 2 properties
var q = {};           // Empty object; no properties
q.x = 2; q.y = 1;     // Now q has the same props as p
```

Object literals can be nested. For example:

```
var rectangle = { upperLeft:  { x: 2, y: 2 },
                  lowerRight: { x: 4, y: 5 } };
```

The expressions in object and array initializers are evaluated each time the object initializer is evaluated, and they need not have constant values: they can be arbitrary JavaScript expressions. Also, the property names in object literals may be quoted strings rather than identifiers (this is useful to specify property names that are reserved words or are otherwise not legal identifiers):

```
var side = 1;
var square = { "ul": { x: p.x, y: p.y },
               'lr': { x: p.x + side, y: p.y + side}};
```

Property Access

A property access expression evaluates to the value of an object property or an array element. JavaScript defines two syntaxes for property access:

```
expression . identifier
expression [ expression ]
```

The first style of property access is an expression followed by a period and an identifier. The expression specifies the object, and the identifier specifies the name of the desired property. The second style of property access follows the first expression (the object or array) with another expression in square brackets. This second expression specifies the name of the desired property or the index of the desired array element. Here are some concrete examples:

```
var o = {x:1,y:{z:3}}; // Example object
var a = [o,4,[5,6]];   // An array that contains o
o.x         // => 1: property x of expression o
o.y.z       // => 3: property z of expression o.y
o["x"]      // => 1: property x of object o
a[1]        // => 4: element at index 1 of expression a
a[2]["1"]   // => 6: element at index 1 of expression a[2]
a[0].x      // => 1: property x of expression a[0]
```

The *.identifier* syntax is the simpler of the two property access options, but notice that it can only be used when the property you want to access has a name that is a legal identifier, and when you know the name when you write the program. If the property name is a reserved word or includes spaces or punctuation characters, or when it is a number (for arrays), you must use the square bracket notation. Square brackets are also used when the property name is not static but is itself the result of a computation.

Function Definition

A function definition expression defines a JavaScript function, and the value of such an expression is the newly defined function. In a sense, a function definition expression is a "function literal" in the same way that an object initializer is an "object literal." A function definition expression typically consists of the keyword **function** followed by a comma-separated list of zero or more identifiers (the parameter names) in parentheses and a block of JavaScript code (the function body) in curly braces. For example:

```
// This function returns the square of its argument
var square = function(x) { return x * x; }
```

Functions can also be defined using a function statement rather than a function expression. Complete details on function definition are in Chapter 7.

Invocation

An *invocation expression* is JavaScript's syntax for calling (or executing) a function or method. It starts with a function expression that identifies the function to be called. The function expression is followed by an open parenthesis, a comma-separated list of zero or more argument expressions, and a close parenthesis. Some examples:

```
f(0)            // f is the function; 0 is the argument.
Math.max(x,y,z) // Function Math.max; arguments x, y & z.
a.sort()        // Function a.sort; no arguments.
```

When an invocation expression is evaluated, the function expression is evaluated first, and then the argument expressions are evaluated to produce a list of argument values. If the value of the function expression is not a function, a TypeError is thrown. Next, the argument values are assigned, in order, to the parameter names specified when the function was defined, and then the body of the function is executed. If the function uses a **return** statement to return a value, then that value becomes the value of the invocation expression. Otherwise, the value of the invocation expression is **undefined**.

Every invocation expression includes a pair of parentheses and an expression before the open parenthesis. If that expression is a property access expression, then the invocation is known as a *method invocation*. In method invocations, the object or array that is the subject of the property access becomes the value of the `this` parameter while the body of the function is being executed. This enables an object-oriented programming paradigm in which functions (known by their OO name, "methods") operate on the object of which they are part. See Chapter 8 for details.

Object Creation

An *object creation expression* creates a new object and invokes a function (called a constructor) to initialize the properties of that object. Object creation expressions are like invocation expressions except that they are prefixed with the keyword `new`:

```
new Object()
new Point(2,3)
```

If no arguments are passed to the constructor function in an object creation expression, the empty pair of parentheses can be omitted:

```
new Object
new Date
```

When an object creation expression is evaluated, JavaScript first creates a new empty object, just like the one created by the object initializer {}. Next, it invokes the specified function with the specified arguments, passing the new object as the value of the `this` keyword. The function can then use `this` to initialize the properties of the newly created object. Functions written for use as constructors do not return a value, and the value of the object creation expression is the newly created and initialized object. If a constructor does return an object value, that value becomes the value of the object creation expression and the newly created object is discarded.

Operators

Operators are used for JavaScript's arithmetic expressions, comparison expressions, logical expressions, assignment expressions, and more. Table 3-1 summarizes JavaScript's operators.

Table 3-1. JavaScript operators

Operator	Operation	Types
++	Pre- or post-increment	lval→num
--	Pre- or post-decrement	lval→num
-	Negate number	num→num
+	Convert to number	num→num
~	Invert bits	int→int
!	Invert boolean value	bool→bool
delete	Remove a property	lval→bool
typeof	Determine type of operand	any→str
void	Return undefined value	any→undef
*, /, %	Multiply, divide, remainder	num,num→num
+, -	Add, subtract	num,num→num
+	Concatenate strings	str,str→str
<<	Shift left	int,int→int
>>	Shift right with sign extension	int,int→int
>>>	Shift right with zero extension	int,int→int
<, <=,>, >=	Compare in numeric order	num,num→bool
<, <=,>, >=	Compare in alphabetic order	str,str→bool
instanceof	Test object class	obj,func→bool
in	Test whether property exists	str,obj→bool
==	Test for equality	any,any→bool
!=	Test for inequality	any,any→bool
===	Test for strict equality	any,any→bool
!==	Test for strict inequality	any,any→bool
&	Compute bitwise AND	int,int→int
^	Compute bitwise XOR	int,int→int

Operator	Operation	Types
|	Compute bitwise OR	int,int→int
&&	Compute logical AND	any,any→any
||	Compute logical OR	any,any→any
?:	Choose 2nd or 3rd operand	bool,any,any→any
=	Assign to a variable or property	lval,any→any
*=, /=, %=, +=, -=, &=, ^=, |=, <<=, >>=, >>>=	Operate and assign	lval,any→any
,	Discard 1st operand, return 2nd	any,any→any

The operators listed in Table 3-1 are arranged in order from high precedence to low precedence, with horizontal lines separating groups of operators at the same precedence level. Operator precedence controls the order in which operations are performed. Operators with higher precedence (nearer the top of the table) are performed before those with lower precedence (nearer to the bottom).

Consider the following expression:

```
w = x + y*z;
```

The multiplication operator * has a higher precedence than the addition operator +, so the multiplication is performed before the addition. Furthermore, the assignment operator = has the lowest precedence, so the assignment is performed after all the operations on the right side are completed.

Operator precedence can be overridden with the explicit use of parentheses. To force the addition in the previous example to be performed first, write:

```
w = (x + y)*z;
```

Note that property access and invocation expressions have higher precedence than any of the operators listed in Table 3-1. Consider this expression:

```
typeof my.functions[x](y)
```

Although typeof is one of the highest-priority operators, the typeof operation is performed on the result of the two property accesses and the function invocation.

In practice, if you are at all unsure about the precedence of your operators, the simplest thing to do is to use parentheses to make the evaluation order explicit. The rules that are important to know are these: multiplication and division are performed before addition and subtraction, and assignment has very low precedence and is almost always performed last.

Some operators work on values of any type, but most expect their operands to be of a specific type, and most operators return (or evaluate to) a value of a specific type. The Types column in Table 3-1 specifies operand types (before the arrow) and result type (after the arrow) for the operators. The number of types before the arrow indicates the *arity* of the operator: *unary* operators have one operand, *binary* operators have two, and the *ternary* ?: operator has three.

Some operators behave differently depending on the type of the operands used with them. Most notably, the + operator adds numeric operands but concatenates string operands. Similarly, the comparison operators such as < perform comparison in numerical or alphabetical order depending on the type of the operands.

Notice that the assignment operators and a few of the other operators listed in Table 3-1 expect an operand of type lval. This is an abbreviation for *lvalue*: a historical term that means "an expression that can legally appear on the left side of an assignment expression." In JavaScript, variables, properties of objects, and elements of arrays are lvalues.

Evaluating a simple expression like 2 * 3 never affects the state of your program, and any future computation your program performs will be unaffected by that evaluation. Some expressions, however, have *side effects*, and their evaluation may affect the result of future evaluations. The assignment operators

are the most obvious example: if you assign a value to a variable
or property, that changes the value of any expression that uses
that variable or property. The ++ and -- increment and decrement operators are similar, since they perform an implicit assignment. The `delete` operator also has side effects: deleting a
property is like (but not the same as) assigning `undefined` to the
property.

Arithmetic Operators

This section covers the operators that perform arithmetic or
other numerical manipulations on their operands.

Multiplication (*)

    Computes the product of its two operands.

Division (/)

    The / operator divides its first operand by its second. If
    you are used to programming languages that distinguish
    between integer and floating-point numbers, you might
    expect to get an integer result when you divide one integer
    by another. In JavaScript, however, all numbers are
    floating-point, so all division operations have floating-
    point results: 5/2 evaluates to 2.5, not 2. Division by zero
    yields positive or negative infinity, and 0/0 evaluates to
    NaN: neither of these cases raises an error.

Modulo (%)

    The % operator computes the first operand modulo the
    second operand. In other words, it returns the remainder
    after whole-number division of the first operand by the
    second operand. The sign of the result is the same as the
    sign of the first operand. For example, 5 % 2 evaluates to
    1 and -5 % 2 evaluates to -1. This operator is typically used
    with integer operands, but it also works for floating-point
    values. For example, 6.5 % 2.1 evaluates to 0.2.

Addition (+)

    The binary + operator adds numeric operands or concat-
    enates string operands:

```
1 + 2                      // => 3
"hello" + " " + "there"    // => "hello there"
"1" + "2"                  // => "12"
1 + 2 + " blind mice";     // => "3 blind mice"
1 + (2 + " blind mice");   // => "12 blind mice"
```

When the values of both operands are numbers, or are
both strings, then it is obvious what the + operator does.
In any other case, however, type conversion is necessary,
and the operation to be performed depends on the conversion performed. The conversion rules for + give priority
to string concatenation: if either of the operands is a string
or an object that converts to a string, the other operand is
converted to a string and concatenation is performed. Addition is performed only if neither operand is string-like.

Subtraction (-)

Subtracts the value of the right-hand operand from the
value of the left-hand operand.

In addition to the binary operators listed above, JavaScript also
defines some unary operators for arithmetic. Unary operators
modify the value of a single operand to produce a new value:

Unary plus (+)

The unary plus operator converts its operand to a number
(or to NaN) and returns that converted value. When used
with an operand that is already a number, it doesn't do
anything.

Unary minus (-)

When - is used as a unary operator, it converts its operand
to a number, if necessary, and then changes the sign of the
result.

Increment (++)

The ++ operator increments (i.e., adds 1 to) its single
operand, which must be an lvalue (a variable, an element
of an array, or a property of an object). The operator converts its operand to a number, adds 1 to that number, and
assigns the incremented value back into the variable, element, or property.

The return value of the ++ operator depends on its position relative to the operand. When used before the operand, where it is known as the pre-increment operator, it increments the operand and evaluates to the incremented value of that operand. When used after the operand, where it is known as the post-increment operator, it increments its operand but evaluates to the *unincremented* value of that operand. Consider the difference between these two lines of code:

```
var i = 1, j = ++i;    // i and j are both 2
var i = 1, j = i++;    // i is 2, j is 1
```

This operator, in both its pre- and post-increment forms, is most commonly used to increment a counter that controls a **for** loop ("for" on page 61).

Decrement (--)

The -- operator expects an lvalue operand. It converts the value of the operand to a number, subtracts 1, and assigns the decremented value back to the operand. Like the ++ operator, the return value of -- depends on its position relative to the operand. When used before the operand, it decrements and returns the decremented value. When used after the operand, it decrements the operand but returns the *undecremented* value.

The bitwise operators perform low-level manipulation of the bits in the binary representation of numbers. These operators are not commonly used in JavaScript programming, and if you are not familiar with the binary representation of decimal integers, you can probably skip this section. The bitwise operators expect integer operands and behave as if those values were represented as 32-bit integers rather than 64-bit floating-point values. These operators convert their operands to numbers, if necessary, and then coerce the numeric values to 32-bit integers by dropping any fractional part and any bits beyond the 32nd. The shift operators require a right-side operand between 0 and 31.

Bitwise AND (&)

The & operator performs a Boolean AND operation on each bit of its integer arguments. A bit is set in the result only if the corresponding bit is set in both operands. For example, 0x1234 & 0x00FF evaluates to 0x0034.

Bitwise OR (|)

The | operator performs a Boolean OR operation on each bit of its integer arguments. A bit is set in the result if the corresponding bit is set in one or both of the operands. For example, 0x1234 | 0x00FF evaluates to 0x12FF.

Bitwise XOR (^)

The ^ operator performs a Boolean exclusive OR operation on each bit of its integer arguments. Exclusive OR means that either operand one is **true** or operand two is **true**, but not both. A bit is set in this operation's result if a corresponding bit is set in one (but not both) of the two operands. For example, 0xFF00 ^ 0xF0F0 evaluates to 0x0FF0.

Bitwise NOT (~)

The ~ operator is a unary operator that appears before its single integer operand. It operates by reversing all bits in the operand. Because of the way signed integers are represented in JavaScript, applying the ~ operator to a value is equivalent to changing its sign and subtracting 1. For example, ~0x0F evaluates to 0xFFFFFFF0, or –16.

Shift left (<<)

The << operator moves all bits in its first operand to the left by the number of places specified in the second operand. For example, in the operation a << 1, the first bit (the ones bit) of a becomes the second bit (the twos bit), the second bit of a becomes the third, etc. A zero is used for the new first bit, and the value of the 32nd bit is lost. Shifting a value left by one position is equivalent to multiplying by 2, shifting two positions is equivalent to multiplying by 4, and so on. For example, 7 << 2 evaluates to 28.

Shift right with sign (>>)

> The >> operator moves all bits in its first operand to the right by the number of places specified in the second operand (an integer between 0 and 31). Bits that are shifted off the right are lost. The bits filled in on the left depend on the sign bit of the original operand, in order to preserve the sign of the result. If the first operand is positive, the result has zeros placed in the high bits; if the first operand is negative, the result has ones placed in the high bits. Shifting a value right one place is equivalent to dividing by 2 (discarding the remainder), shifting right two places is equivalent to integer division by 4, and so on. For example, 7 >> 1 evaluates to 3, and -7 >> 1 evaluates to –4.

Shift right with zero fill (>>>)

> The >>> operator is just like the >> operator, except that the bits shifted in on the left are always zero, regardless of the sign of the first operand. For example, -1 >> 4 evaluates to –1, but -1 >>> 4 evaluates to 0x0FFFFFFF.

Relational Operators

JavaScript's relational operators test for a relationship (such as "equals," "less than," or "property of") between two values and return true or false depending on whether that relationship exists. Relational expressions always evaluate to a boolean value, and that value is often used to control the flow of program execution in if, while, and for statements (see Chapter 4).

JavaScript supports =, ==, and === operators. Be sure you understand the differences between these assignment, equality, and strict equality operators, and be careful to use the correct one when coding! Although it is tempting to read all three operators "equals," it may help to reduce confusion if you read "gets or is assigned" for =, "is equal to" for ==, and "is strictly equal to" for ===.

Strict equality (===)

The === operator is known as the strict equality operator (or sometimes the identity operator), and it checks whether its two operands are "identical" using a strict definition of sameness that does not include any type conversion of the operands. If the operands have different types, they are not equal. If both operands are primitive types and their values are the same, they are equal. If both operands refer to the same object, array, or function, they are equal. If they refer to different objects they are not equal, even if both objects have identical properties. Similarly, two arrays that have the same elements in the same order are not equal to each other. The only quirk in the behavior of this operator is that it considers the not-a-number value NaN to be not equal to any other value, including itself!

Strict inequality (!==)

The !== operator is the exact opposite of the === operator: it returns **false** if two values are strictly equal to each other and returns **true** otherwise.

Loose equality (==)

The == operator (with two equals signs instead of three) is like the strict equality operator, but it is less strict. If the values of the two operands are not the same type, it attempts some type conversions and tries the comparison again. This operator considers null and undefined to be equal, and this is often a helpful type conversion. But other conversions performed by == are more surprising. The following comparisons all evaluate to **true**:

```
1 == "1"
true == 1
"1" == true
false == 0
[] == 0
```

Loose inequality (!=)

The != operator is the exact opposite of the == operator: it returns **false** if two values are loosely equal to each other and returns **true** otherwise.

The comparison operators test the relative order (numerical or alphabetical) of their two operands. Operands that are not numbers or strings are converted to numbers or strings. These operators treat strings as sequences of 16-bit integer values, and that string comparison is just a numerical comparison of the values in the two strings. Note in particular that string comparison is case-sensitive, and all capital ASCII letters are "less than" all lowercase ASCII letters. This rule can cause confusing results if you do not expect it. For example, according to the < operator, the string "Zoo" comes before the string "aardvark":

Less than (<)

The < operator evaluates to **true** if its first operand is less than its second operand; otherwise it evaluates to **false**.

Greater than (>)

The > operator evaluates to **true** if its first operand is greater than its second operand; otherwise it evaluates to **false**.

Less than or equal (<=)

The <= operator evaluates to **true** if its first operand is less than or equal to its second operand; otherwise it evaluates to **false**.

Greater than or equal (>=)

The >= operator evaluates to **true** if its first operand is greater than or equal to its second operand; otherwise it evaluates to **false**.

The final two relational operators are in and instanceof:

Property existence (in)

The in operator expects a left-side operand that is or can be converted to a string. It expects a right-side operand that is an object. It evaluates to **true** if the left-side value

is the name of a property of the right-side object. For
example:

```
var p = { x:1, y:1 };
"x" in p // => true: p has a property named "x".
"z" in p // => false: p has no "z" property.
"toString" in p // => true: p inherits toString.

var a = [7,8,9];
"0" in a // => true: a has an element "0"
1 in a // => true: numbers are converted
```

Object type (`instanceof`)

The `instanceof` operator expects a left-side operand that
is an object and a right-side operand that identifies a class
of objects. The operator evaluates to **true** if the left-side
object is an instance of the right-side class and evaluates
to **false** otherwise. Chapter 8 explains that, in JavaScript,
classes of objects are defined by the constructor function
that initializes them. Thus, the right-side operand of
`instanceof` should be a function. Here are examples:

```
var d = new Date();
d instanceof Date;   // => true
d instanceof Object; // => true
d instanceof Number; // => false
var a = [1, 2, 3];
a instanceof Array;  // => true
a instanceof Object; // => true
```

Logical Expressions

The logical operators &&, ||, and ! perform Boolean algebra
and are often used in conjunction with the relational operators
to combine two relational expressions into one more complex
expression. In order to fully understand them, remember that
null, undefined, 0, "", and NaN are all "falsy" values that work
like the boolean value false. All other values, including all objects and arrays, are "truthy" and work like true.

The && operator can be understood at three different levels. At
the simplest level, when used with boolean operands, &&

performs the Boolean AND operation on the two values: it returns `true` if and only if both its first operand *and* its second operand are `true`. If one or both of these operands is `false`, it returns `false`.

`&&` is often used as a conjunction to join two relational expressions:

```
// true if (and only if) x and y are both 0
x == 0 && y == 0
```

Relational expressions always evaluate to `true` or `false`, so when used like this, the `&&` operator itself returns `true` or `false`. Relational operators have higher precedence than `&&` (and `||`), so expressions like these can safely be written without parentheses.

But `&&` does not require that its operands be boolean values. The second level at which `&&` can be understood is as a Boolean AND operator for truthy and falsy values. If both operands are truthy, the operator returns a truthy value. Otherwise, one or both operands must be falsy, and the operator returns a falsy value. In JavaScript, any expression or statement that expects a boolean value will work with a truthy or falsy value, so the fact that `&&` does not always evaluate to `true` or `false` does not cause practical problems.

Notice that the description above says that the operator returns "a truthy value" or "a falsy value," but does not specify what that value is. For that, we need to describe `&&` at the third and final level. This operator starts by evaluating its first operand, the expression on its left. If the value on the left is falsy, the value of the entire expression must also be falsy, so `&&` simply returns the value on the left and does not even evaluate the expression on the right.

On the other hand, if the value on the left is truthy, then the overall value of the expression depends on the value on the right-hand side. If the value on the right is truthy, then the overall value must be truthy, and if the value on the right is falsy, then the overall value must be falsy. So when the value on the left is truthy, the **&&** operator evaluates and returns the value on the right:

```
var o = { x : 1 };
var p = null;
o && o.x // => 1: o is truthy, so return o.x
p && p.x // => null: p is falsy, so don't eval p.x
```

It is important to understand that **&&** may or may not evaluate its right-side operand. In the code above, the variable **p** is set to **null**, and the expression **p.x** would, if evaluated, cause a TypeError. But the code uses **&&** in an idiomatic way so that **p.x** is evaluated only if **p** is truthy—not **null** or **undefined**.

The **||** operator performs the Boolean OR operation on its two operands. If one or both operands is truthy, it returns a truthy value. If both operands are falsy, it returns a falsy value.

Although the **||** operator is most often used simply as a Boolean OR operator, it, like the **&&** operator, has more complex behavior. It starts by evaluating its first operand, the expression on its left. If the value of this first operand is truthy, it returns that truthy value. Otherwise, it evaluates its second operand, the expression on its right, and returns the value of that expression.

An idiomatic usage of this operator is to select the first truthy value in a set of alternatives:

```
// If max_width is defined, use that.  Otherwise look
// for a value in the preferences object.  If that is
// not defined use a hard-coded constant.
var max = max_width || preferences.max_width || 500;
```

This idiom is often used in function bodies to supply default values for parameters:

```
// Copy the properties of o to p, and return p
function copy(o, p) {
    // If no object passed for p, use a new one
    p = p || {};
    // function body goes here
}
```

The **!** operator is a unary operator; it is placed before a single operand. Its purpose is to invert the boolean value of its operand. For example, if x is truthy, !x evaluates to **false**. If x is falsy, then !x is **true**. Since ! always evaluates to **true** or **false**, you can convert any value x to its equivalent boolean value by applying this operator twice: !!x.

As a unary operator, ! has high precedence and binds tightly. If you want to invert the value of an expression like p && q, you need to use parentheses: !(p && q).

Assignment Expressions

JavaScript uses the = operator to assign a value to a variable, object property, or array element. For example:

```
i = 0    // Set the variable i to 0.
o.x = 1  // Set the property x of object o to 1.
```

The = operator expects its left-side operand to be an lvalue: a variable or object property or array element. It expects its right-side operand to be an arbitrary value of any type. The value of an assignment expression is the value of the right-side operand. As a side effect, the = operator assigns the value on the right to the variable or property on the left so that future references to the variable or property evaluate to the value.

The assignment operator has right-to-left associativity, which means that when multiple assignment operators appear in an expression, they are evaluated from right to left. Thus, you can write code like this to assign a single value to multiple variables:

```
i = j = k = 0;        // Initialize 3 variables to 0
```

Besides the normal = assignment operator, JavaScript supports a number of other assignment operators that provide shortcuts by combining assignment with some other operation. For example, the += operator performs addition and assignment. The following expression:

```
total += sales_tax
```

is equivalent to this one:

```
total = total + sales_tax
```

As you might expect, the += operator works for numbers or strings. For numeric operands, it performs addition and assignment; for string operands, it performs concatenation and assignment.

Similar operators include -=, *=, &=, and so on.

Evaluation Expressions

Like many interpreted languages, JavaScript has the ability to interpret strings of JavaScript source code, evaluating them to produce a value. JavaScript does this with the global function eval():

```
eval("3+2")    // => 5
```

Dynamic evaluation of strings of source code is a powerful language feature that is almost never necessary in practice. If you find yourself using eval(), you should think carefully about whether you really need to use it. Technically, eval() is a function, but it is covered here because in many ways it behaves more like an operator.

eval() expects one argument. If you pass any value other than a string, it simply returns that value. If you pass a string, it attempts to parse the string as JavaScript code, throwing a SyntaxError if it fails. If it successfully parses the string, then it evaluates the code and returns the value of the last expression or statement in the string, or undefined if the last expression or statement had no value. If the evaluated string throws an exception, that exception propagates from the call to eval().

The key thing about eval() (when invoked like this) is that it uses the variable environment of the code that calls it. That is, it looks up the values of variables and defines new variables and functions in the same way that local code does. If a function defines a local variable x and then calls eval("x"), it will obtain the value of the local variable. If it calls eval("x=1"), it changes the value of the local variable. And if the function calls `eval("var y = 3;")`, it has declared a new local variable y. Similarly, a function can declare a local function with code like this:

```
eval("function f() { return x+1; }");
```

`eval()` has a very unusual restriction (which is required to enable JavaScript interpreters to run efficiently): it only behaves the way described above when called with its original name "eval." Since it is technically a function, we can assign it to another variable. And if we invoke it using that other variable, it behaves differently: when invoked by any other name, `eval()` evaluates the string as if it were top-level global code. The evaluated code can define new global variables or global functions, and it can set global variables, but it cannot use or modify any variables local to the calling function.

Before IE9, IE differs from other browsers: it does not do a global eval when `eval()` is invoked by a different name. IE does define a global function named `execScript()` that executes its string argument as if it were a top-level script. Unlike `eval()`, however, `execScript()` always returns null.

ECMAScript 5 strict mode imposes further restrictions on the behavior of `eval()`. When `eval()` is called from strict mode code, or when the string of code to be evaluated itself begins with a "use strict" directive, then `eval()` does a local eval with a private variable environment. This means that in strict mode, evaluated code can query and set local variables, but it cannot define new variables or functions in the local scope. Furthermore, strict mode makes `eval()` even more operator-like by effectively making "eval" into a reserved word.

Miscellaneous Operators

JavaScript supports a number of other miscellaneous operators, described in the following sections.

The Conditional Operator (?:)

The conditional operator is the only ternary operator (three operands) in JavaScript. This operator is sometimes written ?:, although it does not appear quite that way in code. Because this operator has three operands, the first goes before the ?, the second goes between the ? and the :, and the third goes after the :. It is used like this:

```
x > 0 ? x : -x // The absolute value of x
```

The operands of the conditional operator may be of any type. The first operand is evaluated and interpreted as a boolean. If the value of the first operand is truthy, then the second operand is evaluated, and its value is returned. Otherwise, if the first operand is falsy, then the third operand is evaluated and its value is returned. Only one of the second and third operands is evaluated, never both.

While you can achieve similar results using the **if** statement ("if" on page 56), the ?: operator often provides a handy shortcut. Here is a typical usage, which checks to be sure that a property is defined (and has a meaningful, truthy value) and uses it if so, or provides a default value if not:

```
greeting = "hello " + (user.name ? user.name : "there");
```

The typeof Operator

typeof is a unary operator that is placed before its single operand, which can be of any type. Its value is a string that specifies the type of the operand. The following table specifies the value of the **typeof** operator for any JavaScript value:

x	typeof x
undefined	"undefined"
null	"object"
true or false	"boolean"
any number or NaN	"number"

x	typeof x
any string	`"string"`
any function	`"function"`
any nonfunction object	`"object"`

You might use the `typeof` operator in an expression like this:

```
(typeof value == "string") ? "'" + value + "'" : value
```

The delete Operator

`delete` is a unary operator that attempts to delete the object property or array element specified as its operand. (If you are a C++ programmer, note that the `delete` keyword in JavaScript is nothing like the `delete` keyword in C++.) Like the assignment, increment, and decrement operators, `delete` is typically used for its property deletion side effect, and not for the value it returns. Some examples:

```
var o = {x:1, y:2}, a = [1,2,3];
delete o.x;  // Delete a property of o
"x" in o     // => false: the property does not exist
delete a[2]; // Delete the last element of the array
2 in a       // => false: array element 2 doesn't exist
```

The void Operator

`void` is a unary operator that appears before its single operand, which may be of any type. This operator is unusual and very infrequently used: it evaluates its operand, then discards the value and returns `undefined`. Since the operand value is discarded, using the `void` operator makes sense only if the operand has side effects.

The Comma Operator (,)

The comma operator is a binary operator whose operands may be of any type. It evaluates its left operand, evaluates its right operand, and then returns the value of the right operand. The left-hand expression is always evaluated, but its value is discarded, which means that it only makes sense to use the comma operator when the left-hand expression has side effects. The only situation in which the comma operator is commonly used is with a **for** loop ("for" on page 61) that has multiple loop variables:

```
// The first comma below is part of the syntax of the
// var statement. The second comma is the comma operator:
// it lets us squeeze 2 expressions (i++ and j--) into a
// statement (the for loop) that expects 1.
for(var i=0,j=10; i < j; i++,j--)
    console.log(i+j);
```

CHAPTER 4

Statements

Chapter 3 described expressions as JavaScript phrases. By that analogy, *statements* are JavaScript sentences or commands. Just as English sentences are terminated and separated from each other with periods, JavaScript statements are terminated with semicolons ("Optional Semicolons" on page 3). Expressions are *evaluated* to produce a value, but statements are *executed* to make something happen.

One way to "make something happen" is to evaluate an expression that has side effects. Expressions with side effects, such as assignments and function invocations, can stand alone as statements, and when used this way they are known as *expression statements*. A similar category of statements are the *declaration statements* that declare new variables and define new functions.

JavaScript programs are nothing more than a sequence of statements to execute. By default, the JavaScript interpreter executes these statements one after another in the order they are written. Another way to "make something happen" is to alter this default order of execution, and JavaScript has a number of statements or *control structures* that do just this:

- *Conditionals* are statements like `if` and `switch` that make the JavaScript interpreter execute or skip other statements depending on the value of an expression.

- *Loops* are statements like `while` and `for` that execute other statements repetitively.
- *Jumps* are statements like `break`, `return`, and `throw` that cause the interpreter to jump to another part of the program.

Table 4-1 summarizes JavaScript statement syntax, and the sections that follow it describe each statement in more detail.

Table 4-1. JavaScript statement syntax

Statement	Syntax	Purpose
break	`break [label];`	Exit from the innermost loop or `switch` or from named enclosing statement
case	`case expression:`	Label a statement within a `switch`
continue	`continue [label];`	Begin next iteration of the innermost loop or the named loop
debugger	`debugger;`	Debugger breakpoint
default	`default:`	Label the default statement within a `switch`
do/while	`do statement while (expression);`	An alternative to the `while` loop
empty	`;`	Do nothing
for	`for(init; test; incr) statement`	An easy-to-use loop
for/in	`for (var in object) statement`	Enumerate the properties of *object*
function	`function name([param[,...]]) { body }`	Declare a function named *name*
if/else	`if (expr) statement1 [else statement2]`	Execute *statement1* or *statement2*
label	`label: statement`	Give *statement* the name *label*
return	`return [expression];`	Return a value from a function

Statement	Syntax	Purpose
switch	switch (*expression*) { *statements* }	Multiway branch to case or default: labels
throw	throw *expression*;	Throw an exception
try	try {*statements*}	Handle exceptions
	[catch { *statements* }]	
	[finally { *statements* }]	
use strict	"use strict";	Apply strict mode restrictions to script or function
var	var *name* [= *expr*] [,...];	Declare and initialize one or more variables
while	while (*expression*) *statement*	A basic loop construct
with	with (*object*) *statement*	Extend the scope chain (forbidden in strict mode)

Expression Statements

The simplest kinds of statements in JavaScript are expressions that have side effects. This sort of statement was shown in Chapter 3. Assignment statements are one major category of expression statements. For example:

```
greeting = "Hello " + name;
i *= 3;
```

The increment and decrement operators, ++ and --, are related to assignment statements. These have the side effect of changing a variable value, just as if an assignment had been performed:

```
counter++;
```

The delete operator has the important side effect of deleting an object property. Thus, it is almost always used as a statement, rather than as part of a larger expression:

```
delete o.x;
```

Function calls are another major category of expression statements. For example:

```
alert(greeting);
window.close();
```

These client-side function calls are expressions, but they have side effects that affect the web browser and are used here as statements.

Compound and Empty Statements

A *statement block* combines multiple statements into a single *compound statement*. A statement block is simply a sequence of statements enclosed within curly braces. Thus, the following lines act as a single statement and can be used anywhere that JavaScript expects a single statement:

```
{
    x = Math.PI;
    cx = Math.cos(x);
    console.log("cos(π) = " + cx);
}
```

Combining statements into larger statement blocks is extremely common in JavaScript programming. Just as expressions often contain subexpressions, many JavaScript statements contain substatements. Formally, JavaScript syntax usually allows a single substatement. For example, the while loop syntax includes a single statement that serves as the body of the loop. Using a statement block, you can place any number of statements within this single allowed substatement.

A compound statement allows you to use multiple statements where JavaScript syntax expects a single statement. The *empty statement* is the opposite: it allows you to include no statements where one is expected.

The empty statement looks like this:

```
;
```

The JavaScript interpreter takes no action when it executes an empty statement. The empty statement is occasionally useful when you want to create a loop that has an empty body:

```
// Initialize the elements of a to 0
for(i = 0; i < a.length; a[i++] = 0) /* empty */;
```

Declaration Statements

The var and function are *declaration statements*—they declare or define variables and functions. These statements define identifiers (variable and function names) that can be used elsewhere in your program and assign values to those identifiers. Declaration statements don't do much themselves, but by creating variables and functions they, in an important sense, define the meaning of the other statements in your program.

var

The var statement declares a variable or variables. Here's the syntax:

```
var name_1 [ = value_1] [ ,..., name_n [= value_n]]
```

The var keyword is followed by a comma-separated list of variables to declare; each variable in the list may optionally have an initializer expression that specifies its initial value. For example:

```
var i;                           // One simple variable
var j = 0;                       // One var, one value
var p, q;                        // Two variables
var greeting = "hello" + name;   // A complex initializer
var x = 2, y = x*x;              // Second var uses first
var x = 2,                       // Multiple variables...
    f = function(x) { return x*x }, // each on its
    y = f(x);                    // own line
```

If a `var` statement appears within the body of a function, it defines local variables, scoped to that function. When `var` is used in top-level code, it declares global variables, visible throughout the JavaScript program.

If no initializer is specified for a variable with the `var` statement, the variable's initial value is `undefined`.

Note that the `var` statement can also appear as part of the `for` and `for/in` loops:

```
for(var i = 0; i < 10; i++) console.log(i);
for(var i = 0, j=10; i < 10; i++,j--) console.log(i*j);
for(var i in o) console.log(i);
```

function

The `function` keyword is used to define functions. We saw it in function definition expressions in "Function Definition" on page 26. It can also be used in statement form. Consider the following two functions:

```
// Expression assigned to a variable
var f = function(x) { return x+1; }
// The statement form includes the variable name
function f(x) { return x+1; }
```

A function declaration statement has the following syntax:

```
function funcname([arg1 [, arg2 [..., argn]]]) {
    statements
}
```

funcname is an identifier that names the function being declared. The function name is followed by a comma-separated list of parameter names in parentheses. These identifiers can be used within the body of the function to refer to the argument values passed when the function is invoked.

The body of the function is composed of any number of JavaScript statements, contained within curly braces. These statements are not executed when the function is defined. Instead, they are associated with the new function object for execution when the function is invoked.

Here are some more examples of function declarations:

```javascript
function hypotenuse(x, y) {
    return Math.sqrt(x*x + y*y);
}

function factorial(n) {         // A recursive function
    if (n <= 1) return 1;
    return n * factorial(n - 1);
}
```

Function declaration statements may appear in top-level Java-Script code, or they may be nested within other functions. When nested, however, function declarations may only appear at the top level of the function they are nested within. That is, function definitions may not appear within `if` statements, `while` loops, or any other statements.

Function declaration statements differ from function definition expressions in that they include a function name. Both forms create a new function object, but the function declaration statement also declares the function name as a variable and assigns the function object to it. Like variables declared with `var`, functions defined with function definition statements are implicitly "hoisted" to the top of the containing script or function, so that all functions in a script or all nested functions in a function are declared before any other code is run. This means that you can invoke a JavaScript function before you declare it.

Conditionals

Conditional statements execute or skip other statements depending on the value of a specified expression. These statements are the decision points of your code, and they are also sometimes known as "branches." If you imagine a JavaScript interpreter following a path through your code, the conditional statements are the places where the code branches into two or more paths and the interpreter must choose which path to follow.

if

The `if` statement is the fundamental control statement that allows JavaScript to execute statements conditionally. This statement has two forms. The first is:

```
if (expression)
    statement
```

In this form, *expression* is evaluated. If the resulting value is truthy, *statement* is executed. If *expression* is falsy, *statement* is not executed:

```
if (username == null) // If username is null or undefined,
    username = "John Doe"; // define it
```

Note that the parentheses around the *expression* are a required part of the syntax for the `if` statement.

The second form of the `if` statement introduces an `else` clause that is executed when *expression* is `false`. Its syntax is:

```
if (expression)
    statement1
else
    statement2
```

This form of the statement executes *statement1* if *expression* is truthy and executes `statement2` if *expression* is falsy. For example:

```
if (n == 1) {
    console.log("You have 1 new message.");
}
else {
    console.log("You have " + n + " new messages.");
}
```

else if

The `if/else` statement evaluates an expression and executes one of two pieces of code, depending on the outcome. But what about when you need to execute one of many pieces of code? One way to do this is with an `else if` statement. `else if` is not really a JavaScript statement, but simply a frequently used programming idiom that results when repeated if/else statements are used:

```
if (n == 1) {
    // Execute code block #1
}
else if (n == 2) {
    // Execute code block #2
}
else if (n == 3) {
    // Execute code block #3
}
else {
    // If all else fails, execute block #4
}
```

There is nothing special about this code. It is just a series of if statements, where each following if is part of the else clause of the previous statement. Using the else if idiom is preferable to, and more legible than, writing these statements out in their syntactically equivalent, fully nested form:

```
if (n == 1) {
    // Execute code block #1
}
else {
    if (n == 2) {
        // Execute code block #2
    }
    else {
        if (n == 3) {
            // Execute code block #3
        }
        else {
            // If all else fails, execute block #4
        }
    }
}
```

switch

An if statement causes a branch in the flow of a program's execution, and you can use the else if idiom to perform a multiway branch. This is not the best solution, however, when all of the branches depend on the value of the same expression.

In this case, it is wasteful to repeatedly evaluate that expression in multiple **if** statements.

The **switch** statement handles exactly this situation. The **switch** keyword is followed by an expression in parentheses and a block of code in curly braces:

```
switch(expression) {
    statements
}
```

However, the full syntax of a **switch** statement is more complex than this. Various locations in the block of code are labeled with the **case** keyword followed by an expression and a colon. **case** is like a labeled statement, except that instead of giving the labeled statement a name, it associates an expression with the statement. When a **switch** executes, it computes the value of *expression* and then looks for a **case** label whose expression evaluates to the same value (where sameness is determined by the === operator). If it finds one, it starts executing the block of code at the statement labeled by the **case**. If it does not find a **case** with a matching value, it looks for a statement labeled **default:**. If there is no **default:** label, the **switch** statement skips the block of code altogether.

The following **switch** statement is equivalent to the repeated **if/else** statements shown in the previous section:

```
switch(n) {
  case 1:                      // Start here if n === 1
    // Execute code block #1.
    break;                     // Stop here
  case 2:                      // Start here if n === 2
    // Execute code block #2.
    break;                     // Stop here
  case 3:                      // Start here if n === 3
    // Execute code block #3.
    break;                     // Stop here
  default:                     // If all else fails...
    // Execute code block #4.
    break;                     // stop here
}
```

Note the **break** keyword used at the end of each **case** in the code above. The **break** statement, described later in this chapter, causes the interpreter to break out of the **switch** statement and continue with the statement that follows it. The **case** clauses in a **switch** statement specify only the *starting point* of the desired code; they do not specify any ending point. In the absence of **break** statements, a **switch** statement begins executing its block of code at the **case** label that matches the value of its *expression* and continues executing statements until it reaches the end of the block. Usually you will want to end every **case** with a **break** or **return** statement.

Here is a more realistic example of the **switch** statement; it converts a value to a string in a way that depends on the type of the value:

```
function convert(x) {
    switch(typeof x) {
      case 'number': // Convert to a hexadecimal integer
        return x.toString(16);
      case 'string': // Enclose it in quotes
        return '"' + x + '"';
      default:        // Any other type
        return String(x);
    }
}
```

Note that in the two previous examples, the **case** keywords are followed by number and string literals, respectively. This is how the **switch** statement is most often used in practice, but note that the ECMAScript standard allows each **case** to be followed by an arbitrary expression.

Loops

To understand conditional statements, we imagined the JavaScript interpreter following a branching path through your source code. The *looping statements* are those that bend that path back upon itself to repeat portions of your code. JavaScript has four looping statements: **while**, **do/while**, **for**, and **for/in**.

while

The while statement is JavaScript's basic loop. It has the following syntax:

```
while (expression)
    statement
```

To execute a while statement, the interpreter first evaluates
expression. If the value of the expression is falsy, then the interpreter skips over the *statement* that serves as the loop body
and moves on to the next statement in the program. If, on the
other hand, the *expression* is truthy, the interpreter executes
the *statement* and repeats, jumping back to the top of the loop
and evaluating *expression* again. Another way to say this is that
the interpreter executes *statement* repeatedly *while* the *expres
sion* is truthy. Note that you can create an infinite loop with
the syntax while(true).

Here is an example of a while loop that prints the numbers
from 0 to 9:

```
var count = 0;
while (count < 10) {
    console.log(count);
    count++;
}
```

As you can see, the variable count starts off at 0 and is incremented each time the body of the loop runs. Once the loop has
executed 10 times, the expression becomes false (i.e., the variable count is no longer less than 10), the while statement finishes, and the interpreter can move on to the next statement in
the program.

do/while

The do/while loop is like a while loop, except that the loop
expression is tested at the bottom of the loop rather than at the
top. This means that the body of the loop is always executed
at least once. The syntax of this relatively uncommon loop is:

```
do
    statement
while (expression);
```

Here's an example of a **do/while** loop:

```
function printArray(a) {
    var len = a.length, i = 0;
    if (len == 0)
        console.log("Empty Array");
    else {
        do {
            console.log(a[i]);
        } while (++i < len);
    }
}
```

for

The **for** statement simplifies loops that follow a common pattern. Most loops have a counter variable of some kind. This variable is initialized before the loop starts and is tested before each iteration of the loop. Finally, the counter variable is incremented or otherwise updated at the end of the loop body, just before the variable is tested again. In this kind of loop, the initialization, the test, and the update are the three crucial manipulations of a loop variable. The **for** statement encodes each of these three manipulations as an expression and makes those expressions an explicit part of the loop syntax:

```
for(initialize ; test ; increment)
    statement
```

initialize, *test*, and *increment* are three expressions (separated by semicolons) that are responsible for initializing, testing, and incrementing the loop variable. Putting them all in the first line of the loop makes it easy to understand what a **for** loop is doing and prevents mistakes such as forgetting to initialize or increment the loop variable.

The simplest way to explain how a **for** loop works is to show the equivalent **while** loop:

```
initialize;
  while(test) {
      statement
      increment;
  }
```

In other words, the *initialize* expression is evaluated once, before the loop begins. To be useful, this expression must have side effects (usually an assignment). JavaScript also allows *initialize* to be a **var** variable declaration statement so that you can declare and initialize a loop counter at the same time. The *test* expression is evaluated before each iteration and controls whether the body of the loop is executed. If *test* evaluates to a truthy value, the *statement* that is the body of the loop is executed. Finally, the *increment* expression is evaluated. Again, this must be an expression with side effects in order to be useful. Generally, either it is an assignment expression, or it uses the ++ or -- operators.

We can print the numbers from 0 to 9 with a **for** loop like the following. Contrast it with the equivalent **while** loop shown above:

```
for(var count = 0; count < 10; count++)
    console.log(count);
```

for/in

The **for/in** statement uses the **for** keyword, but it is a completely different kind of loop than the regular **for** loop. A **for/in** loop looks like this:

```
for (variable in object)
    statement
```

variable typically names a variable, but it may also be a **var** statement that declares a single variable. *object* is an expression that evaluates to an object. As usual, *statement* is the statement or statement block that serves as the body of the loop.

It is easy to use a regular **for** loop to iterate through the elements of an array:

```
// Assign array indexes to variable i
for(var i = 0; i < a.length; i++)
    console.log(a[i]); // Print each array element
```

The `for/in` loop makes it easy to do the same for the properties of an object:

```
// Assign property names of o to variable p
for(var p in o)
    console.log(o[p]); // Print each property
```

To execute a `for/in` statement, the JavaScript interpreter first evaluates the *object* expression and then executes the body of the loop once for each enumerable property of the resulting object. Before each iteration, however, the interpreter assigns the name of the property to the *variable*.

The `for/in` loop does not actually enumerate all properties of an object, only the *enumerable* properties (see "Property Attributes" on page 87). The various built-in methods defined by core JavaScript are not enumerable. All objects have a `toString()` method, for example, but the `for/in` loop does not enumerate this `toString` property. In addition to built-in methods, many other properties of the built-in objects are nonenumerable. All properties and methods defined by your code are enumerable, however. (But in ECMAScript 5, you can make them nonenumerable using techniques explained in "Property Attributes" on page 87.)

The ECMAScript specification does not describe the order in which the `for/in` loop enumerates the properties of an object. In practice, however, JavaScript implementations from all major browser vendors enumerate the properties of simple objects in the order in which they were defined, with older properties enumerated first. If an object was created as an object literal, its enumeration order is the same order that the properties appear in the literal. Note that this enumeration order does not apply to all objects. In particular, if an object includes array index properties, those properties may be enumerated in numeric order rather than in creation order.

Jumps

Another category of JavaScript statements are *jump statements*. As the name implies, these cause the JavaScript interpreter to jump to a new location in the source code. The **break** statement makes the interpreter jump to the end of a loop or other statement. **continue** makes the interpreter skip the rest of the body of a loop and jump back to the top of a loop to begin a new iteration. JavaScript allows statements to be named, or *labeled*, and the **break** and **continue** can identify the target loop or other statement label. The **return** statement makes the interpreter jump from a function invocation back to the code that invoked it and also supplies the value for the invocation. The **throw** statement raises, or "throws," an exception and is designed to work with the **try/catch/finally** statement, which establishes a block of exception handling code.

Labeled Statements

Any statement may be *labeled* by preceding it with an identifier and a colon:

```
identifier: statement
```

By labeling a statement, you give it a name that you can use to refer to it elsewhere in your program. You can label any statement, although it is only useful to label statements that have bodies, such as loops and conditionals. By giving a loop a name, you can use **break** and **continue** statements inside the body of the loop to exit the loop or to jump directly to the top of the loop to begin the next iteration. **break** and **continue** are the only JavaScript statements that use statement labels; they are covered later in this chapter. Here is an example of a labeled **while** loop and a **continue** statement that uses the label.

```
mainloop: while(token != null) {
    // Code omitted...
    continue mainloop; // Jump to top of the named loop
    // More code omitted...
}
```

break

The **break** statement, used alone, causes the innermost enclosing loop or **switch** statement to exit immediately. Its syntax is simple:

```
break;
```

Because it causes a loop or **switch** to exit, this form of the **break** statement is legal only if it appears inside one of these statements.

You've already seen examples of the **break** statement within a **switch** statement. In loops, it is typically used to exit prematurely when, for whatever reason, there is no longer any need to complete the loop. When a loop has complex termination conditions, it is often easier to implement some of these conditions with **break** statements rather than trying to express them all in a single loop expression. The following code searches the elements of an array for a particular value. The loop terminates in the normal way when it reaches the end of the array; it terminates with a **break** statement if it finds what it is looking for in the array:

```
for(var i = 0; i < a.length; i++) {
    if (a[i] == target) break;
}
```

Although it is rarely used in practice, JavaScript allows the **break** keyword to be followed by a statement label (just the identifier, with no colon):

```
break labelname;
```

When **break** is used with a label, it jumps to the end of, or terminates, the enclosing statement that has the specified label. It is a syntax error to use **break** in this form if there is no enclosing statement with the specified label. With this form of the **break** statement, the named statement need not be a loop or **switch**: **break** can "break out of" any enclosing statement.

continue

The continue statement is similar to the break statement. Instead of exiting a loop, however, continue restarts a loop at the next iteration. The continue statement's syntax is just as simple as the break statement's:

```
continue;
```

The continue statement can also be used with a label:

```
continue labelname;
```

The continue statement, in both its labeled and unlabeled forms, can be used only within the body of a loop. Using it anywhere else causes a syntax error.

The following example shows an unlabeled continue statement being used to skip the rest of the current iteration of a loop when an error occurs:

```
for(i = 0; i < data.length; i++) {
    if (isNaN(data[i])) continue; // Skip non-numbers.
    total += data[i];
}
```

Like the break statement, the continue statement can be used in its labeled form within nested loops, when the loop to be restarted is not the immediately enclosing loop.

return

Recall that function invocations are expressions and that all expressions have values. A return statement within a function specifies the value of invocations of that function. Here's the syntax of the return statement:

```
return expression;
```

A return statement may appear only within the body of a function. It is a syntax error for it to appear anywhere else. When the return statement is executed, the function that contains it returns the value of *expression* to its caller. For example:

```
function square(x) { return x*x; } // Returns x squared
square(2) // This invocation evaluates to 4
```

With no **return** statement, a function invocation simply executes each of the statements in the function body in turn until it reaches the end of the function, and then returns to its caller. In this case, the invocation expression evaluates to **undefined**. The **return** statement can also be used without an *expression* to make the function return **undefined** before it reaches the end of its body. For example:

```
function display_object(o) {
    // Return immediately if o is null or undefined.
    if (!o) return;
    // Rest of function goes here...
}
```

throw

An *exception* is a signal that indicates that some sort of exceptional condition or error has occurred. To *throw* an exception is to signal such an error or exceptional condition. To *catch* an exception is to handle it—to take whatever actions are necessary or appropriate to recover from the exception. In JavaScript, exceptions are thrown whenever a runtime error occurs and whenever the program explicitly throws one using the **throw** statement. Exceptions are caught with the **try/catch/finally** statement, which is described next.

The **throw** statement has the following syntax:

```
throw expression;
```

expression may evaluate to a value of any type. You might throw a number that represents an error code or a string that contains a human-readable error message. The Error class and its subclasses are used when the JavaScript interpreter itself throws an error, and you can use them as well. An Error object has a **name** property that specifies the type of error and a **mes sage** property that holds the string passed to the constructor function (see the Error class in the reference section). Here is

an example function that throws an Error object when invoked
with an invalid argument:

```
function factorial(x) {
    // If x is invalid, throw an exception!
    if (x < 0) throw new Error("x must not be negative");
    // Otherwise, compute a value and return normally
    for(var f = 1; x > 1; f *= x, x--) /* empty */ ;
    return f;
}
```

When an exception is thrown, the JavaScript interpreter immediately stops normal program execution and jumps to the
nearest exception handler. Exception handlers are written using the catch clause of the try/catch/finally statement, which
is described in the next section. If the block of code in which
the exception was thrown does not have an associated catch
clause, the interpreter checks the next highest enclosing block
of code to see if it has an exception handler associated with it.
This continues until a handler is found. If an exception is
thrown in a function that does not contain a try/catch/
finally statement to handle it, the exception propagates up to
the code that invoked the function. In this way, exceptions
propagate up through the lexical structure of JavaScript methods and up the call stack. If no exception handler is ever found,
the exception is treated as an error and is reported to the user.

try/catch/finally

The try/catch/finally statement is JavaScript's exception
handling mechanism. The try clause of this statement simply
defines the block of code whose exceptions are to be handled.
The try block is followed by a catch clause, which is a block
of statements that are invoked when an exception occurs anywhere within the try block. The catch clause is followed by a
finally block containing cleanup code that is guaranteed to be
executed, regardless of what happens in the try block. Both
the catch and finally blocks are optional, but a try block must
be accompanied by at least one of these blocks. The try,
catch, and finally blocks all begin and end with curly braces.

These braces are a required part of the syntax and cannot be omitted, even if a clause contains only a single statement.

The following code illustrates the syntax and purpose of the `try/catch/finally` statement:

```
try {
    // Normally, this code runs from the top of the block
    // to the bottom without problems. But it can
    // sometimes throw an exception, either directly, with
    // a throw statement, or indirectly, by calling a
    // method that throws an exception.
}
catch (e) {
    // The statements in this block are executed if, and
    // only if, the try block throws an exception. These
    // statements can use the local variable e to refer
    // to the Error object or other value that was thrown.
    // This block may handle the exception somehow, may
    // ignore the exception by doing nothing, or may
    // rethrow the exception with throw.
}
finally {
    // This block contains statements that are always
    // executed, regardless of what happens in the try
    // block. They are executed when the try block
    // terminates:
    //    1) normally, after reaching the bottom
    //    2) because of a break, continue, or return
    //    3) with an exception handled by a catch above
    //    4) with an uncaught exception that is propagating
}
```

Note that the `catch` keyword is followed by an identifier in parentheses. This identifier is like a function parameter. When an exception is caught, the value associated with the exception (an Error object, for example) is assigned to this parameter. Unlike regular variables, the identifier associated with a `catch` clause has block scope—it is only defined within the `catch` block.

Here is a realistic example of the `try/catch` statement. It uses the `factorial()` method defined in the previous section and the client-side JavaScript methods `prompt()` and `alert()` for input and output:

```
try {
    // Ask the user to enter a number
    var n = Number(prompt("Enter an number", ""));
    // Compute the factorial of the number,
    // assuming the input is valid.
    var f = factorial(n);
    // Display the result
    alert(n + "! = " + f);
}
catch (ex) {    // We end up here on invalid input.
    alert(ex);  // Tell the user what the error is.
}
```

Miscellaneous Statements

This section describes the remaining three JavaScript statements—with, debugger, and use strict.

with

When JavaScript looks up the value of a variable, it first looks at the variables defined within the current function, then (if the function is nested) at variables defined in enclosing functions and finally at global variables. The with statement temporarily alters the way variables are looked up by specifying an object whose properties should be treated as if they were variables. It has the following syntax:

```
with (object)
    statement
```

This statement executes *statement* somewhat as if it was the body of a nested function and the properties of *object* were parameters passed to that function.

The with statement is forbidden in strict mode (see "use strict") and should be considered deprecated in nonstrict mode: avoid using it whenever possible. JavaScript code that uses with is difficult to optimize and is likely to run much more slowly than the equivalent code written without the with statement.

---

debugger

The **debugger** statement normally does nothing. If, however, a debugger program is available and is running, then an implementation may (but is not required to) perform some kind of debugging action. In practice, this statement acts like a breakpoint: execution of JavaScript code stops and you can use the debugger to print variables' values, examine the call stack, and so on. Suppose, for example, that you are getting an exception in your function f() because it is being called with an undefined argument, and you can't figure out where this call is coming from. To help you in debugging this problem, you might alter f() so that it begins like this:

```
function f(o) {
  if (o === undefined) debugger; // Debug hook
  // The rest of the function goes here.
}
```

Now, when f() is called with no argument, execution will stop, and you can use the debugger to inspect the call stack and find out where this incorrect call is coming from.

The **debugger** statement was formally added to the language by ECMAScript 5, but it has been implemented by major browser vendors for quite some time.

"use strict"

"use strict" is a *directive* introduced in ECMAScript 5. Directives are not statements (but are close enough that "use strict" is documented here). "use strict" does not involve any JavaScript keywords: it is simply a JavaScript string literal expression, and is ignored by ECMAScript 3 interpreters. When placed at the beginning of a script or of a function body, however, it has special meaning to an ECMAScript 5 interpreter.

The purpose of a "use strict" directive is to indicate that the code that follows (in the script or function) is *strict code*. Strict code is executed in *strict mode*. The strict mode of

ECMAScript 5 is a restricted subset of the language that fixes a few important language deficiencies and provides stronger error checking and increased security. The most important differences between strict mode and non-strict mode are the following:

- The `with` statement is not allowed in strict mode.

- In strict mode, all variables must be declared: a ReferenceError is thrown if you assign a value to an identifier that is not a declared variable, parameter, or property of the global object. (In nonstrict mode, this implicitly declares a global variable by adding a new property to the global object.)

- In strict mode, functions invoked as functions (rather than as methods) have a `this` value of `undefined`. (In nonstrict mode, functions invoked as functions are always passed the global object as their `this` value.) This difference can be used to determine whether an implementation supports strict mode:

    ```
    var hasStrictMode = (function() {
        "use strict";
         return this === undefined;
    }());
    ```

- In strict mode, assignments to nonwritable properties and attempts to create new properties on nonextensible objects throw a TypeError. (In nonstrict mode, these attempts fail silently.) Similarly, in strict mode, an attempt to delete a nonconfigurable property or a nonproperty value throws a TypeError or SyntaxError. (In nonstrict mode, the attempt fails and the `delete` expression evaluates to `false`.)

- In strict mode, code passed to `eval()` cannot declare variables or define functions in the caller's scope as it can in nonstrict mode. Instead, variable and function definitions live in a new scope created for the `eval()`. This scope is discarded when the `eval()` returns.

- In strict mode, octal integer literals (beginning with a 0 that is not followed by an x) are not allowed. (In nonstrict mode, some implementations allow octal literals.)

- In strict mode, the identifiers `eval` and `arguments` are treated like keywords, and you are not allowed to change their value.

CHAPTER 5

Objects

JavaScript's fundamental datatype is the *object*. An object is a composite value: it aggregates multiple values (primitive values or other objects) and allows you to store and retrieve those values by name. An object is an unordered collection of *properties*, each of which has a name and a value. Property names are strings, so we can say that objects map strings to values. This string-to-value mapping goes by various names: you are probably already familiar with the fundamental data structure under the name "hash," "hashtable," "dictionary," or "associative array." An object is more than a simple string-to-value map, however. In addition to maintaining its own set of properties, a JavaScript object also inherits the properties of another object, known as its "prototype." The methods of an object are typically inherited properties, and this "prototypal inheritance" is a key feature of JavaScript.

JavaScript objects are dynamic—properties can usually be added and deleted—but they can be used to simulate the static objects and "structs" of statically typed languages. They can also be used (by ignoring the value part of the string-to-value mapping) to represent sets of strings.

Any value in JavaScript that is not a string, a number, `true`, `false`, `null`, or `undefined` is an object.

Objects are *mutable* and are manipulated by reference rather than by value: if the variable x refers to an object, and the code **var** y = x; is executed, the variable y holds a reference to the same object, not a copy of that object. Any modifications made to the object through the variable y are also visible through the variable x.

Creating Objects

Objects can be created with object literals, with the new keyword, and (in ECMAScript 5) with the Object.create() function.

Object Literals

The easiest way to create an object is to include an object literal in your JavaScript code. An *object literal* is a comma-separated list of colon-separated name:value pairs, enclosed within curly braces. A property name is a JavaScript identifier or a string literal (the empty string is allowed). A property value is any JavaScript expression; the value of the expression (it may be a primitive value or an object value) becomes the value of the property. Here are some examples:

```
var empty = {};          // An object with no properties
var point = { x:0, y:0 }; // Two properties
var point2 = {           // Another object literal
    x:point.x,           // With more complex properties
    y:point.y+1
};
var book = { // Nonidentifier property names are quoted
    "main title": "JavaScript", // space in property name
    'sub-title': "Pocket Ref",  // punctuation in name
    "for": "all audiences",     // reserved word name
};
```

Creating Objects with new

The new operator creates and initializes a new object. The new keyword must be followed by a function invocation. A function used in this way is called a *constructor* and serves to initialize a newly created object. Core JavaScript includes built-in constructors for native types. For example:

```
var o = new Object();      // An empty object: same as {}.
var a = new Array();       // An empty array: same as [].
var d = new Date();        // A Date for the current time.
var r = new RegExp("js");  // A pattern matching object.
```

In addition to these built-in constructors, it is common to define your own constructor functions to initialize newly created objects. Doing so is covered in Chapter 8.

Prototypes

Before we can cover the third object creation technique, we must pause for a moment to explain prototypes. Every Java-Script object has a second JavaScript object (or null, but this is rare) associated with it. This second object is known as a prototype, and the first object inherits properties from the prototype.

All objects created by object literals have the same prototype object, and we can refer to this prototype object in JavaScript code as Object.prototype. Objects created using the new keyword and a constructor invocation use the value of the proto type property of the constructor function as their prototype. So the object created by new Object() inherits from Object.pro totype just as the object created by {} does. Similarly, the object created by new Array() uses Array.prototype as its prototype, and the object created by new Date() uses Date.prototype as its prototype.

Object.prototype is one of the rare objects that has no prototype: it does not inherit any properties. Other prototype objects are normal objects that do have a prototype. All of the built-in constructors (and most user-defined constructors) have a prototype that inherits from Object.prototype. For example, Date.prototype inherits properties from Object.prototype, so a Date object created by new Date() inherits properties from both `Date.prototype` and `Object.prototype`. This linked series of prototype objects is known as a *prototype chain*.

An explanation of how property inheritance works is in "Property Inheritance" on page 80. We'll learn how to query the prototype of an object in "The prototype Attribute" on page 90. And Chapter 8 explains the connection between prototypes and constructors in more detail: it shows how to define new "classes" of objects by writing a constructor function and setting its `prototype` property to the prototype object to be used by the "instances" created with that constructor.

Object.create()

ECMAScript 5 defines a method, `Object.create()`, that creates a new object, using its first argument as the prototype of that object. `Object.create()` also takes an optional second argument that describes the properties of the new object. This second argument is covered in "Property Attributes" on page 87.

`Object.create()` is a static function, not a method invoked on individual objects. To use it, simply pass the desired prototype object:

```
// o1 inherits properties x and y.
var o1 = Object.create({x:1, y:2});
```

You can pass `null` to create a new object that does not have a prototype, but if you do this, the newly created object will not inherit anything, not even basic methods like `toString()` (which means it won't work with the + operator either):

```
// o2 inherits no properties or methods.
var o2 = Object.create(null);
```

If you want to create an ordinary empty object (like the object returned by {} or new `Object()`), pass `Object.prototype`:

```
// o3 is like {} or new Object().
var o3 = Object.create(Object.prototype);
```

The ability to create a new object with an arbitrary prototype (put another way: the ability to create an "heir" for any object) is a powerful one, and we can simulate it in ECMAScript 3 with a function like the one in Example 5-1.

Example 5-1. Creating a new object that inherits from a prototype

```
// inherit() returns a newly created object that inherits
// properties from the prototype object p.  It uses the
// ECMAScript 5 function Object.create() if it is defined,
// and otherwise falls back to an older technique.
function inherit(p) {
    if (p == null)         // p must be a non-null
        throw TypeError();
    if (Object.create)     // Use Object.create()
        return Object.create(p); //   if it is defined.
    var t = typeof p;      // Make sure p is an object
    if (t !== "object" && t !== "function")
        throw TypeError();
    function f() {};       // Define a dummy constructor.
    f.prototype = p;       // Set its prototype property
    return new f();        // Use it to create an "heir" of p.
}
```

The code in the `inherit()` function will make more sense after we've covered constructors in Chapter 8.

Properties

The most important part of an object are its properties. The sections that follow explain them in detail.

Querying and Setting Properties

To obtain the value of a property, you can use the dot (.) or square bracket ([]) operators described in "Property Access" on page 26. The left-hand side should be an expression whose value is an object. If using the dot operator, the right-hand must be a simple identifier that names the property. If using square brackets, the value within the brackets must be an expression that evaluates to a string (or number) that contains the desired property name:

```
// Get the "author" property of the book.
var author = book.author;
// Get the "surname" property of the author.
var name = author.surname
// Get the "main title" property of the book.
var title = book["main title"]
```

To create or set a property, use a dot or square brackets as you would to query the property, but put them on the left-hand side of an assignment expression:

```
// Create an "edition" property of book.
book.edition = 6;
// Set the "main title" property.
book["main title"] = "ECMAScript";
```

Property Inheritance

JavaScript objects have a set of "own properties," and they also inherit a set of properties from their prototype object. To understand this, we must consider property access in more detail. The examples in this section use the **inherit()** function from Example 5-1 in order to create objects with specified prototypes.

Suppose you query the property x in the object o. If o does not have an own property with that name, the prototype object of o is queried for the property x. If the prototype object does not have an own property by that name, but has a prototype itself, the query is performed on the prototype of the prototype. This continues until the property x is found or until an object with a **null** prototype is searched. As you can see, the *prototype* attribute of an object creates a chain or linked list from which properties are inherited:

```
// o inherits object methods from Object.prototype
var o = {}
o.x = 1;                // and has an own property x.
// p inherits properties from o and Object.prototype
var p = inherit(o);
p.y = 2;                // and has an own property y.
```

```
// q inherits properties from p, o, and Object.prototype
var q = inherit(p);
q.z = 3;                // and has an own property z.
// toString is inherited from Object.prototype
var s = q.toString();
// x and y are inherited from o and p
q.x + q.y               // => 3
```

Now suppose you assign to the property x of the object o. If o already has an own (noninherited) property named x, then the assignment simply changes the value of this existing property. Otherwise, the assignment creates a new property named x on the object o. If o previously inherited the property x, that inherited property is now hidden by the newly created own property with the same name.

Deleting Properties

The delete operator ("The delete Operator" on page 46) removes a property from an object. Its single operand should be a property access expression. Surprisingly, delete does not operate on the value of the property but on the property itself:

```
delete book.author;       // book now has no author.
delete book["main title"]; // or a "main title", either.
```

The delete operator only deletes own properties, not inherited ones. (To delete an inherited property, you must delete it from the prototype object in which it is defined. Doing this affects every object that inherits from that prototype.)

Testing Properties

JavaScript objects can be thought of as sets of properties, and it is often useful to be able to test for membership in the set—to check whether an object has a property with a given name. You can do this with the in operator, with the hasOwnProp erty() and propertyIsEnumerable() methods, or simply by querying the property.

The **in** operator expects a property name (as a string) on its left side and an object on its right. It returns **true** if the object has an own property or an inherited property by that name:

```
var o = { x: 1 }
"x" in o;          // true: o has an own property "x"
"y" in o;          // false: o doesn't have a property "y"
"toString" in o; // true: o inherits a toString property
```

The hasOwnProperty() method of an object tests whether that object has an own property with the given name. It returns **false** for inherited properties:

```
var o = { x: 1 }
o.hasOwnProperty("x"); // true: o has an own property x
o.hasOwnProperty("y"); // false: o has no property y
// toString is an inherited property
o.hasOwnProperty("toString"); // false
```

The propertyIsEnumerable() method refines the hasOwnProperty() test. It returns **true** only if the named property is an own property and its *enumerable* attribute is **true**. Certain built-in properties are not enumerable. Properties created by normal JavaScript code are enumerable unless you've used one of the ECMAScript 5 methods shown later to make them nonenumerable:

```
var o = inherit({ y: 2 });
o.x = 1;
// o has an own enumerable property x
o.propertyIsEnumerable("x");  // true
// y is inherited, not own
o.propertyIsEnumerable("y");  // false
// false: the toString method is not enumerable
Object.prototype.propertyIsEnumerable("toString");
```

Instead of using the **in** operator, it is often sufficient to simply query the property and use !== to make sure it is not undefined:

```
var o = { x: 1 }
o.x !== undefined;        // true: o has a property x
o.y !== undefined;        // false: o has no property y
o.toString !== undefined; // true: o inherits it
```

There is one thing the **in** operator can do that the simple property access technique shown above cannot do. **in** can distinguish between properties that do not exist and properties that exist but have been set to undefined. Consider this code:

```
var o = { x: undefined }
o.x !== undefined // false: property is undefined
o.y !== undefined // false: property doesn't exist
"x" in o          // true:  property exists
"y" in o          // false: property doesn't exist
delete o.x;       // Delete the property x
"x" in o          // false: it doesn't exist anymore
```

Enumerating Properties

Instead of testing for the existence of individual properties, we sometimes want to iterate through or obtain a list of all the properties of an object. This is usually done with the for/in loop, although ECMAScript 5 provides two handy alternatives.

The for/in loop was covered in "for/in" on page 62. It runs the body of the loop once for each enumerable property (own or inherited) of the specified object, assigning the name of the property to the loop variable. Built-in methods that objects inherit are not enumerable, but the properties that your code adds to objects are enumerable (unless you use one of the functions described later to make them nonenumerable). For example:

```
// This object has three enumerable own properties
var o = {x:1, y:2, z:3};
// Its inherited methods are not enumerable:
o.propertyIsEnumerable("toString") // => false
// This loop prints x, y and z but not toString
for(p in o) console.log(p);
```

Some utility libraries add new methods (or other properties) to Object.prototype so that they are inherited by, and available to, all objects. Prior to ECMAScript 5, however, there is no way to make these added methods nonenumerable, so they are enumerated by for/in loops. To guard against this, you might want to filter the properties returned by for/in. Here are two ways you might do so:

```
for(p in o) {
    if (!o.hasOwnProperty(p)) // Skip inherited props
```

```
        continue;
    }

    for(p in o) {
        if (typeof o[p] === "function") // Skip methods
            continue;
    }
```

Here is a utility function that uses a for/in loop to copy the properties of one object to another:

```
/*
 * Copy the enumerable properties of p to o,
 * and return o. If o and p have a property with the
 * same name, o's property is overwritten.
 */
function extend(o, p) {
    for(prop in p) {          // For all props in p.
        o[prop] = p[prop];    // Add the property to o.
    }
    return o;
}
```

In addition to the for/in loop, ECMAScript 5 defines two functions that enumerate property names. The first is Object.keys(), which returns an array of the names of the enumerable own properties of an object. The second ECMAScript 5 property enumeration function is Object.getOwnProperty Names(). It works like Object.keys() but returns the names of all the own properties of the specified object, not just the enumerable properties.

Serializing Properties and Objects

Object *serialization* is the process of converting an object's state to a string from which it can later be restored. ECMAScript 5 provides the native functions JSON.stringify() and JSON.parse() to serialize and restore JavaScript objects. These functions use the JSON data interchange format (see *http://json .org*). JSON stands for "JavaScript Object Notation," and its syntax is very similar to that of JavaScript object and array literals:

```
o = {x:1, y:[false,null,""]}; // A test object
s = JSON.stringify(o); // '{"x":1,"y":[false,null,""]}'
p = JSON.parse(s);     // p is a deep copy of o
```

The native implementation of these functions in ECMAScript 5 was modeled very closely after the public-domain ECMAScript 3 implementation available at *http://json.org/json2.js*. For practical purposes, the implementations are the same, and you can use these ECMAScript 5 functions in ECMAScript 3 with this *json2.js* module.

Note that JSON syntax is a *subset* of JavaScript syntax, and it cannot represent all JavaScript values. Objects, arrays, strings, finite numbers, true, false, and null are supported and can be serialized and restored.

Property Getters and Setters

We've said that a property has a name and a value. In ECMAScript 5 (and in recent ECMAScript 3 versions of major browsers other than IE) the value may be replaced by one or two methods, known as a *getter* and a *setter*. Properties defined by getters and setters are sometimes known as *accessor properties* to distinguish them from *data properties* that have a simple value.

When a program queries the value of an accessor property, JavaScript invokes the getter method (passing no arguments). The return value of this method becomes the value of the property access expression. When a program sets the value of an accessor property, JavaScript invokes the setter method, passing the value of the right-hand side of the assignment. This method is responsible for "setting," in some sense, the property value. The return value of the setter method is ignored.

The easiest way to define accessor properties is with an extension to the object literal syntax:

```
var o = {
    // An ordinary data property
    data_prop: value,
```

```
    // An accessor property as a pair of functions
    get accessor_prop() { /* return value */ },
    set accessor_prop(value) { /* set value */ }
};
```

Accessor properties are defined as one or two functions whose name is the same as the property name, and with the **func tion** keyword replaced with **get** and/or **set**. Note that no colon is used to separate the name of the property from the functions that access that property, but that a comma is still required after the function body to separate the method from the next method or data property. As an example, consider the following object that represents a 2-D Cartesian point. It has ordinary data properties to represent the x and y coordinates of the point, and it has accessor properties for the equivalent polar coordinates of the point:

```
var p = {
    // x and y are regular read-write data properties.
    x: 1.0,
    y: 1.0,

    // r is a read-write property with getter and setter.
    // Don't forget to put a comma after accessor methods.
    get r() {
        return Math.sqrt(this.x*this.x + this.y*this.y);
    },
    set r(newvalue) {
     var oldvalue = Math.sqrt(this.x*this.x + this.y*this.y);
     var ratio = newvalue/oldvalue;
     this.x *= ratio;
     this.y *= ratio;
    },

    // theta is a read-only accessor property.
    get theta() { return Math.atan2(this.y, this.x); }
};
```

Here is another example of a useful object with an accessor property:

```
// Generate strictly increasing serial numbers
var serialnum = {
    // This data property holds the next serial number.
    // The $ hints that this is a private property.
    $n: 0,
```

```
    // Return the current value and increment it
    get next() { return this.$n++; },

    // Set a new n, but only if it is >= current n.
    set next(n) {
        if (n >= this.$n) this.$n = n;
        else throw "serial number can only be increased";
    }
};
```

Property Attributes

In addition to a name and value, properties have attributes that specify whether they can be written, enumerated, and configured. In ECMAScript 3, there is no way to set these attributes: all properties created by ECMAScript 3 programs are writable, enumerable, and configurable, and there is no way to change this. This section explains the ECMAScript 5 API for querying and setting property attributes.

For the purposes of this section, we are going to consider getter and setter methods of an accessor property to be property attributes. Following this logic, we'll even say that the value of a data property is an attribute as well. Thus, we can say that a property has a name and four attributes. The four attributes of a data property are *value*, *writable*, *enumerable*, and *configurable*. Accessor properties don't have a *value* attribute or a *writable* attribute: their writability is determined by the presence or absence of a setter. So the four attributes of an accessor property are *get*, *set*, *enumerable*, and *configurable*.

The ECMAScript 5 methods for querying and setting the attributes of a property use an object called a *property descriptor* to represent the set of four attributes. A property descriptor object has properties with the same names as the attributes of the property it describes. Thus, the property descriptor object of a data property has properties named `value`, `writable`, `enumerable`, and `configurable`. And the descriptor for an accessor property has `get` and `set` properties instead of `value` and `writable`. The `writable`, `enumerable`, and `configurable` properties are boolean values, and the `get` and `set` properties are function values, of course.

To obtain the property descriptor for a named property of a specified object, call `Object.getOwnPropertyDescriptor()`:

```
// Returns {value: 1, writable:true,
//          enumerable:true, configurable:true}
Object.getOwnPropertyDescriptor({x:1}, "x");

// Query the theta property of the p object from above.
// Returns { get: /*func*/, set:undefined,
//           enumerable:true, configurable:true}
Object.getOwnPropertyDescriptor(p, "theta");
```

As implied by its name, `Object.getOwnPropertyDescriptor()` works only for own properties. To query the attributes of inherited properties, you must explicitly traverse the prototype chain (see `Object.getPrototypeOf()` in "The prototype Attribute" on page 90).

To set the attributes of a property, or to create a new property with the specified attributes, call `Object.defineProperty()`, passing the object to be modified, the name of the property to be created or altered, and the property descriptor object:

```
var o = {};  // Start with no properties at all
// Add a nonenumerable data property x with value 1.
Object.defineProperty(o, "x", { value : 1,
                                writable: true,
                                enumerable: false,
                                configurable: true});

// Check that the property is there but is nonenumerable
o.x;            // => 1
Object.keys(o) // => []

// Now modify the property x so that it is read-only
Object.defineProperty(o, "x", { writable: false });

// Try to change the value of the property
o.x = 2;  // Fails silently or TypeError in strict mode
o.x       // => 1

// The property is still configurable,
// so we can change its value like this:
```

```
Object.defineProperty(o, "x", { value: 2 });
o.x        // => 2

// Now change x to an accessor property
Object.defineProperty(o, "x", {
    get: function() { return 0; }
});
o.x        // => 0
```

The property descriptor you pass to `Object.defineProperty()`
does not have to include all four attributes. If you're creating
a new property, then omitted attributes are taken to be **false**
or **undefined**. If you're modifying an existing property, then the
attributes you omit are simply left unchanged. Note that this
method alters an existing own property or creates a new own
property, but it will not alter an inherited property.

If you want to create or modify more than one property at a
time, use `Object.defineProperties()`. The first argument is the
object that is to be modified. The second argument is an object
that maps the names of the properties to be created or modified
to the property descriptors for those properties. For example:

```
var p = Object.defineProperties({}, {
    x: { value: 1, writable: true,
        enumerable:true, configurable:true },
    y: { value: 1, writable: true,
        enumerable:true, configurable:true },
    r: {
        get: function() {
          return Math.sqrt(this.x*this.x+this.y*this.y)
        },
        enumerable:true,
        configurable:true
    }
});
```

We saw the ECMAScript 5 method `Object.create()` in "Creating Objects" on page 76. We learned there that the first argument to that method is the prototype object for the newly
created object. This method also accepts a second optional
argument, which is the same as the second argument to
`Object.defineProperties()`. If you pass a set of property

descriptors to `Object.create()`, then they are used to add properties to the newly created object.

Object Attributes

Every object has associated *prototype*, *class*, and *extensible* attributes.

The prototype Attribute

An object's *prototype* attribute specifies the object from which it inherits properties. The prototype attribute is set when an object is created. Recall from "Prototypes" on page 77 that objects created from object literals use `Object.prototype` as their prototype. Objects created with `new` use the value of the `proto type` property of their constructor function as their prototype. And objects created with `Object.create()` use the first argument to that function (which may be `null`) as their prototype.

In ECMAScript 5, you can query the prototype of any object by passing that object to `Object.getPrototypeOf()`. There is no equivalent function in ECMAScript 3, but it is sometimes possible to determine the prototype of an object `o` using the expression `o.constructor.prototype`.

To determine whether one object is the prototype of (or is part of the prototype chain of) another object, use the `isPrototy peOf()` method. To find out if `p` is the prototype of `o` write `p.isPrototypeOf(o)`. For example:

```
var p = {x:1};              // Define a prototype object.
var o = Object.create(p); // Inherit from that prototype.
p.isPrototypeOf(o)          // => true: o inherits from p.
Object.prototype.isPrototypeOf(p) // True for any object.
```

Note that `isPrototypeOf()` performs a function similar to the `instanceof` operator.

The class Attribute

An object's *class* attribute is a string that provides information about the type of the object. Neither ECMAScript 3 nor ECMAScript 5 provide any way to set this attribute, and there is only an indirect technique for querying it. The default `toString()` method (inherited from `Object.prototype`) returns a string of the form:

```
[object class]
```

So to obtain the class of an object, you can invoke this `toString()` method on it, and extract the eighth through the second-to-last characters of the returned string. The tricky part is that many objects inherit other, more useful `toString()` methods, and to invoke the correct version of `toString()`, we must do so indirectly, using the `Function.call()` method (see "Indirect Invocation" on page 120). Example 5-2 defines a function that returns the class of any object you pass it.

Example 5-2. A classof() function

```
function classof(o) {
    if (o === null) return "Null";
    if (o === undefined) return "Undefined";
    return Object.prototype.toString.call(o).slice(8,-1);
}
```

The extensible Attribute

The *extensible* attribute of an object specifies whether new properties can be added to the object or not. ECMAScript 5 defines functions for querying and setting the extensibility of an object. To determine whether an object is extensible, pass it to `Object.isExtensible()`. To make an object nonextensible, pass it to `Object.preventExtensions()`.

`Object.seal()` works like `Object.preventExtensions()`, but in addition to making the object nonextensible, it also makes all of the own properties of that object nonconfigurable. This means that new properties cannot be added to the object, and existing properties cannot be deleted or configured. You can use `Object.isSealed()` to determine whether an object is sealed.

`Object.freeze()` locks objects down even more tightly. In addition to making the object nonextensible and its properties nonconfigurable, it also makes all of the object's own data properties read-only. Use `Object.isFrozen()` to determine if an object is frozen.

It is important to understand that there is no way to undo the effects of `Object.preventExtensions()`, `Object.seal()`, and `Object.freeze()`. Also, these functions affect only the object they are passed: they have no effect on the prototype of that object. Finally, note that these three functions all return the object that they are passed, which means that you can use them in nested function invocations:

```
// Create a sealed object with a frozen prototype
// and a nonenumerable property
o = Object.seal(Object.create(Object.freeze({x:1}),
                        {y: { value: 2,
                                writable: true}}));
```

CHAPTER 6

Arrays

An *array* is an ordered collection of values. Each value is called an *element*, and each element has a numeric position in the array, known as its *index*. JavaScript arrays are *untyped*: an array element may be of any type, and different elements of the same array may be of different types. Array elements may even be objects or other arrays, which allows you to create complex data structures, such as arrays of objects and arrays of arrays. JavaScript arrays are *zero-based* and use 32-bit indexes: the index of the first element is 0, and the highest possible index is 4294967294 (2^{32}–2), for a maximum array size of 4,294,967,295 elements. JavaScript arrays are *dynamic*: they grow or shrink as needed and there is no need to declare a fixed size for the array when you create it or to reallocate it when the size changes. Every JavaScript array has a `length` property that specifies the number of elements in the array.

JavaScript arrays are a specialized form of JavaScript object, and array indexes are really little more than property names that happen to be integers. Implementations typically optimize arrays so that access to numerically indexed array elements is faster than access to regular object properties.

Arrays inherit properties from `Array.prototype`, which defines a rich set of array manipulation methods. Most of these methods are *generic*, which means that they work correctly not only for true arrays, but for any "array-like object." In ECMAScript 5, strings behave like arrays of characters.

Creating Arrays

The easiest way to create an array is with an array literal, which is simply a comma-separated list of array elements within square brackets:

```
var empty = [];              // An array with no elements
var primes = [2, 3, 5, 7];   // An array of 5 numbers
var misc = [{}, true, "a"];  // Elements of various types
```

The values in an array literal need not be constants; they may be arbitrary expressions:

```
var base = 1024;
var table = [base, base+1, base+2, base+3];
```

Array literals can contain object literals or other array literals:

```
var b = [[1,{x:1, y:2}], [2, {x:3, y:4}]];
```

If an array literal contains two commas in a row, with no value between, then an element is missing and the array is *sparse*. Missing elements are **undefined**:

```
var count = [1,,3]; // Elements at indexes 0 and 2.
count[1]            // => undefined
var undefs = [,,];  // No elements but length of 2
```

Array literal syntax allows an optional trailing comma, so [1,2,] has a length of 2, not 3.

Another way to create an array is with the **Array()** constructor. You can invoke this constructor in three distinct ways:

• Call it with no arguments:

```
var a = new Array();
```

This method creates an empty array with no elements and is equivalent to the array literal [].

• Call it with a single numeric argument, which specifies a length:

```
var a = new Array(10);
```

This technique creates an array with the specified length. This form of the `Array()` constructor can be used to pre-allocate an array when you know in advance how many elements will be required. Note that no values are stored in the array, and the array index properties "0," "1," and so on are not even defined for the array.

- Explicitly specify two or more array elements or a single nonnumeric element for the array:

```
var a = new Array(5, 4, 3, 2, 1, "testing");
```

In this form, the constructor arguments become the elements of the new array. Using an array literal is almost always simpler than this usage of the `Array()` constructor.

Array Elements and Length

You access an element of an array using the [ ] operator. A reference to the array should appear to the left of the brackets. An arbitrary expression that has (or can be converted to) a nonnegative integer value should be inside the brackets. You can use this syntax to both read and write the value of an element of an array. Thus, the following are all legal:

```
var a = ["world"];  // Start with a one-element array
var value = a[0];   // Read element 0
a[1] = 3.14;        // Write element 1
i = 2;
a[i] = 3;           // Write element 2
a[i + 1] = "hello"; // Write element 3
a[a[i]] = a[0];     // Read 0 and 2, write 3
```

Remember that arrays are a specialized kind of object. The square brackets used to access array elements work just like the square brackets used to access object properties. JavaScript converts the numeric array index you specify to a string—the index 1 becomes the string "1"—then uses that string as a property name.

Every array has a `length` property, and it is this property that makes arrays different from regular JavaScript objects. The `length` property specifies the number of elements in the array (assuming no missing elements). Its value is one more than the highest index in the array:

```
[].length              // => 0: the array has no elements
['a','b','c'].length   // => 3: highest index is 2
```

All arrays are objects, and you can create properties of any name on them. What is special about arrays is that when you use property names that are (or convert to) nonnegative integers less than $2^{32}-1$, the array automatically maintains the value of the `length` property for you.

The `length` property is writable and if you set the `length` property to a nonnegative integer n smaller than its current value, any array elements whose index is greater than or equal to n are deleted from the array:

```
a=[1,2,3,4,5]; // Start with a 5-element array.
a.length = 3; // a is now [1,2,3].
a.length = 0; // Delete all elements.  a is [].
a.length = 5; // Length 5, but no elts, like new Array(5)
```

You can also set the `length` property of an array to a value larger than its current value. Doing this does not actually add any new elements to the array, it simply creates a sparse area at the end of the array.

Iterating Arrays

The most common way to loop through the elements of an array is with a `for` loop ("for" on page 61):

```
var keys = Object.keys(o); // An array of property names
var values = []            // Store property values here
for(var i = 0; i < keys.length; i++) { // For each index
    var key = keys[i];                 // Get the key
    values[i] = o[key];                // Store the value
}
```

In nested loops, or other contexts where performance is critical, you may sometimes see this basic array iteration loop optimized so that the array length is only looked up once rather than on each iteration:

```
for(var i = 0, len = keys.length; i < len; i++) {
    // loop body remains the same
}
```

ECMAScript 5 defines a number of new methods for iterating array elements by passing each one, in index order, to a function that you define. The forEach() method is the most general of these methods:

```
var data = [1,2,3,4,5]; // An array to iterate
var sumOfSquares = 0;    // Update this on each iteration
data.forEach(function(x) { // Pass each elt to this func
                sumOfSquares += x*x; // add up squares
            });
sumOfSquares                // =>55: 1+4+9+16+25
```

Multidimensional Arrays

JavaScript does not support true multidimensional arrays, but you can approximate them with arrays of arrays. To access a value in an array of arrays, simply use the [] operator twice. For example, suppose the variable matrix is an array of arrays of numbers. Every element in matrix[x] is an array of numbers. To access a particular number within this array, you would write matrix[x][y]. Here is a concrete example that uses a two-dimensional array as a multiplication table:

```
// Create a multidimensional array
var table = new Array(10);      // 10 rows of the table
for(var i = 0; i < table.length; i++)
    table[i] = new Array(10); // Each row has 10 columns

// Initialize the array
for(var row = 0; row < table.length; row++) {
    for(col = 0; col < table[row].length; col++) {
        table[row][col] = row*col;
    }
}
```

```
// Use the multidimensional array to compute 5*7
var product = table[5][7];   // 35
```

Array Methods

Arrays have a number of useful methods, demonstrated in the sections below.

join()

The `Array.join()` method converts all the elements of an array to strings and concatenates them, returning the resulting string. You can specify an optional string that separates the elements in the resulting string. If no separator string is specified, a comma is used:

```
var a = [1, 2, 3];
a.join();            // => "1,2,3"
a.join(" ");         // => "1 2 3"
a.join("");          // => "123"
var b = new Array(5); // Length 5 but no elements
b.join('-')          // => '----': a string of 4 hyphens
```

The `Array.join()` method is the inverse of the method `String.split()`, which creates an array by breaking a string into pieces.

reverse()

The `Array.reverse()` method reverses the order of the elements of an array and returns the reversed array. It does this in place; in other words, it doesn't create a new array with the elements rearranged but instead rearranges them in the already existing array:

```
var a = [1,2,3];
a.reverse().join() // => "3,2,1"
a[0]               // => 3: a is now [3,2,1]
```

---

sort()

`Array.sort()` sorts the elements of an array in place and returns the sorted array. When `sort()` is called with no arguments, it sorts the array elements in alphabetical order:

```
var a = new Array("banana", "cherry", "apple");
a.sort();
var s = a.join(", ");  // s == "apple, banana, cherry"
```

If an array contains undefined elements, they are sorted to the end of the array.

To sort an array into some order other than alphabetical, you must pass a comparison function as an argument to `sort()`. This function decides which of its two arguments should appear first in the sorted array. If the first argument should appear before the second, the comparison function should return a number less than zero. If the first argument should appear after the second in the sorted array, the function should return a number greater than zero. And if the two values are equivalent (i.e., if their order is irrelevant), the comparison function should return 0. So, for example, to sort array elements into numerical rather than alphabetical order, you might do this:

```
var a = [33, 4, 1111, 222];
a.sort();                 // Alphabetical: 1111, 222, 33, 4
a.sort(function(a,b) {    // Numerical: 4, 33, 222, 1111
        return a-b; // Returns < 0, 0, or > 0
    });
a.sort(function(a,b) {return b-a}); // Reverse numerical
```

You can perform a case-insensitive alphabetical sort as follows:

```
a = ['ant', 'Bug', 'cat']
a.sort(); // case-sensitive sort: ['Bug','ant',cat']
a.sort(function(s,t) {    // Case-insensitive sort
        var a = s.toLowerCase();
        var b = t.toLowerCase();
        if (a < b) return -1;
        if (a > b) return 1;
        return 0;
    });                   // => ['ant','Bug','cat']
```

concat()

The `Array.concat()` method creates and returns a new array that contains the elements of the original array on which `con cat()` was invoked, followed by each of the arguments to `concat()`. If any of these arguments is itself an array, then it is the array elements that are concatenated, not the array itself. `concat()` does not modify the array on which it is invoked. Here are some examples:

```
var a = [1,2,3];
a.concat(4, 5)          // Returns [1,2,3,4,5]
a.concat([4,5]);        // Returns [1,2,3,4,5]
a.concat([4,5],[6,7])   // Returns [1,2,3,4,5,6,7]
a.concat(4, [5,[6,7]])  // Returns [1,2,3,4,5,[6,7]]
```

slice()

The `Array.slice()` method returns a *slice*, or subarray, of the specified array. Its two arguments specify the start and end of the slice to be returned. The returned array contains the element specified by the first argument and all subsequent elements up to, but not including, the element specified by the second argument. If only one argument is specified, the returned array contains all elements from the start position to the end of the array. If either argument is negative, it specifies an array element relative to the last element in the array. Note that `slice()` does not modify the array on which it is invoked:

```
var a = [1,2,3,4,5];
a.slice(0,3);   // Returns [1,2,3]
a.slice(3);     // Returns [4,5]
a.slice(1,-1);  // Returns [2,3,4]
a.slice(-3,-2); // Returns [3]
```

splice()

The `Array.splice()` method is a general-purpose method for inserting or removing elements from an array. Unlike `slice()` and `concat()`, `splice()` modifies the array on which it is invoked.

The first argument to splice() specifies the array position at which the insertion and/or deletion is to begin. The second argument specifies the number of elements that should be deleted from (spliced out of) the array. If this second argument is omitted, all array elements from the start element to the end of the array are removed. splice() returns an array of the deleted elements, or an empty array if no elements were deleted. For example:

```
var a = [1,2,3,4,5,6,7,8];
a.splice(4);    // Returns [5,6,7,8]; a is [1,2,3,4]
a.splice(1,2);  // Returns [2,3]; a is [1,4]
a.splice(1,1);  // Returns [4]; a is [1]
```

The first two arguments to splice() specify which array elements are to be deleted. These arguments may be followed by any number of additional arguments that specify elements to be inserted into the array, starting at the position specified by the first argument. For example:

```
var a = [1,2,3,4,5];
a.splice(2,0,'a','b'); // =>[]; a is [1,2,'a','b',3,4,5]
a.splice(2,2,3);       // =>['a','b']; a is [1,2,3,3,4,5]
```

Note that, unlike concat(), splice() inserts arrays themselves, not the elements of those arrays.

push() and pop()

The push() and pop() methods allow you to work with arrays as if they were stacks. The push() method appends one or more new elements to the end of an array and returns the new length of the array. The pop() method does the reverse: it deletes the last element of an array, decrements the array length, and returns the value that it removed. Note that both methods modify the array in place rather than produce a modified copy of the array:

```
var stack = [];    // stack: []
stack.push(1,2);   // stack: [1,2]    Returns 2
stack.pop();       // stack: [1]      Returns 2
stack.push(3);     // stack: [1,3]    Returns 2
stack.pop();       // stack: [1]      Returns 3
```

```
stack.push([4,5]);    // stack: [1,[4,5]]  Returns 2
stack.pop()           // stack: [1]        Returns [4,5]
stack.pop();          // stack: []         Returns 1
```

unshift() and shift()

The unshift() and shift() methods behave much like push()
and pop(), except that they insert and remove elements from
the beginning of an array rather than from the end. unshift()
adds an element or elements to the beginning of the array, shifts
the existing array elements up to higher indexes to make room,
and returns the new length of the array. shift() removes and
returns the first element of the array, shifting all subsequent
elements down one place to occupy the newly vacant space at
the start of the array:

```
var a = [];           // a:[]
a.unshift(1);         // a:[1]            Returns: 1
a.unshift(22);        // a:[22,1]         Returns: 2
a.shift();            // a:[1]            Returns: 22
a.unshift(3,[4,5]);   // a:[3,[4,5],1]    Returns: 3
a.shift();            // a:[[4,5],1]      Returns: 3
a.shift();            // a:[1]            Returns: [4,5]
a.shift();            // a:[]             Returns: 1
```

toString()

An array, like any JavaScript object, has a toString() method.
For an array, this method converts each of its elements to a
string (calling the toString() methods of its elements, if necessary) and outputs a comma-separated list of those strings.
Note that the output does not include square brackets or any
other sort of delimiter around the array value. For example:

```
[1,2,3].toString()        // => '1,2,3'
["a", "b", "c"].toString() // => 'a,b,c'
[1, [2,'c']].toString()   // => '1,2,c'
```

ECMAScript 5 Array Methods

ECMAScript 5 defines nine new array methods for iterating, mapping, filtering, testing, reducing, and searching arrays. Most of the methods accept a function as their first argument and invoke that function once for each element (or at least some elements) of the array. In most cases, the function you supply is invoked with three arguments: the value of the array element, the index of the array element, and the array itself. Often, you only need the first of these argument values and can ignore the second and third values. Most of the ECMAScript 5 array methods that accept a function as their first argument accept an optional second argument. If specified, the function is invoked as if it is a method of this second argument. That is, the second argument you pass becomes the value of the **this** keyword inside of the function you pass. The return value of the function you pass is important, but different methods handle the return value in different ways. None of the ECMAScript 5 array methods modify the array on which they are invoked, but the function you pass to the array methods may modify the array, of course.

forEach()

The forEach() method iterates through an array, invoking a function you specify for each element:

```
var data = [1,2,3,4,5];  // Compute the sum of elements
var sum = 0;             // Start at 0
data.forEach(function(value) { sum += value; });
sum                      // => 15

// Now increment each array element
data.forEach(function(v, i, a) { a[i] = v + 1; });
data                     // => [2,3,4,5,6]
```

map()

The map() method passes each element of the array on which it is invoked to the function you specify, and returns a new array containing the values returned by that function:

```
a = [1, 2, 3];
b = a.map(function(x) { return x*x; }); // b is [1, 4, 9]
```

filter()

The filter() method returns an array containing a subset of the elements of the array on which it is invoked. The function you pass to it should be predicate: a function that returns true or false. The predicate is invoked just as for forEach() and map(). If the return value is true, or a value that converts to true, then the element passed to the predicate is a member of the subset and is added to the array that will become the return value:

```
a = [5, 4, 3, 2, 1];
a.filter(function(x) { return x < 3 });   // => [2,1]
a.filter(function(x,i) { return i%2==0 }); // => [5,3,1]
```

every() and some()

The every() and some() methods are array predicates: they apply a predicate function you specify to the elements of the array, and then return true or false.

The every() method is like the mathematical "for all" quantifier ∀: it returns true if and only if your predicate function returns true for all elements in the array:

```
a = [1,2,3,4,5];
// Are all values less than 10?
a.every(function(x) { return x < 10; })    // => true
// Are all values even?
a.every(function(x) { return x%2 === 0; }) // => false
```

The some() method is like the mathematical "there exists" quantifier ∃: it returns true if there exists at least one element in the array for which the predicate returns true, and returns `false` if and only if the predicate returns `false` for all elements of the array:

```
a = [1,2,3,4,5];
// Does a have any even numbers?
a.some(function(x) { return x%2===0; }) // => true
// Does a have any elements that are not numbers?
a.some(isNaN)                           // => false
```

Note that both `every()` and `some()` stop iterating array elements as soon as they know what value to return. Note also that `every()` returns `true` and `some` returns `false` when invoked on an empty array.

reduce(), reduceRight()

The `reduce()` and `reduceRight()` methods combine the elements of an array, using the function you specify, to produce a single value. This is a common operation in functional programming and also goes by the names "inject" and "fold." Examples help illustrate how it works:

```
var a = [1,2,3,4,5]
// Compute the sume of the elements
a.reduce(function(x,y) { return x+y }, 0); // => 15
// Compute the product of the elements
a.reduce(function(x,y) { return x*y }, 1); // => 120
// Compute the largest element
a.reduce(function(x,y) { return (x>y)?x:y; }); // => 5
```

`reduce()` takes two arguments. The first is the function that performs the reduction operation. The task of this reduction function is to somehow combine or reduce two values into a single value, and to return that reduced value. In the examples above, the functions combine two values by adding them, multiplying them, and choosing the largest. The second (optional) argument is an initial value to pass to the function.

Functions used with `reduce()` are different than the functions used with `forEach()` and `map()`. The familiar value, index, and array values are passed as the second, third, and fourth arguments. The first argument is the accumulated result of the reduction so far. On the first call to the function, this first argument is the initial value you passed as the second argument to `reduce()`. On subsequent calls, it is the value returned by the previous invocation of the function. In the first example above, the reduction function is first called with arguments 0 and 1. It adds these and returns 1. It is then called again with arguments 1 and 2 and it returns 3. Next it computes 3+3=6, then 6+4=10, and finally 10+5=15. This final value, 15, becomes the return value of `reduce()`.

You may have noticed that the third call to `reduce()` above has only a single argument: there is no initial value specified. When you invoke `reduce()` like this with no initial value, it uses the first element of the array as the initial value. This means that the first call to the reduction function will have the first and second array elements as its first and second arguments. In the sum and product examples above, we could have omitted the initial value argument.

`reduceRight()` works just like `reduce()`, except that it processes the array from highest index to lowest (right-to-left), rather than from lowest to highest.

indexOf() and lastIndexOf()

`indexOf()` and `lastIndexOf()` search an array for an element with a specified value, and return the index of the first such element found, or −1 if none is found. `indexOf()` searches the array from beginning to end, and `lastIndexOf()` searches from end to beginning:

```
a = [0,1,2,1,0];
a.indexOf(1)        // => 1: a[1] is 1
a.lastIndexOf(1)    // => 3: a[3] is 1
a.indexOf(3)        // => -1: no element has value 3
```

Unlike the other methods described in this section, `indexOf()` and `lastIndexOf()` do not take a function argument. The first argument is the value to search for. The second argument is optional: it specifies the array index at which to begin the search. If this argument is omitted, `indexOf()` starts at the beginning and `lastIndexOf()` starts at the end. Negative values are allowed for the second argument and are treated as an offset from the end of the array.

Array Type

We've seen throughout this chapter that arrays are objects with some special behavior. Given an unknown object, it is often useful to be able to determine whether it is an array or not. In ECMAScript 5, you can do this with the `Array.isArray()` function:

```
Array.isArray([])    // => true
Array.isArray({})    // => false
```

We can write an `isArray()` function that works in any version of JavaScript like this:

```
var isArray = Array.isArray || function(o) {
    var ts = Object.prototype.toString;
    return typeof o === "object" &&
        ts.call(o) === "[object Array]";
};
```

Array-Like Objects

As we've seen, arrays are objects that have a `length` property with special behavior. An "array-like" object is an ordinary JavaScript object that has numeric properties names and a `length` property. These "array-like" objects actually do occasionally appear in practice, and although you cannot directly invoke array methods on them or expect special behavior from the `length` property, you can still iterate through them with the same code you'd use for a true array:

```
// An array-like object
var a = {"0":"a", "1":"b", "2":"c", length:3};
// Iterate through it as if it were a real array
var total = 0;
for(var i = 0; i < a.length; i++)
    total += a[i];
```

Many array algorithms work just as well with array-like objects as they do with real arrays and the JavaScript array methods are purposely defined to be generic, so that they work correctly when applied to array-like objects. Since array-like objects do not inherit from `Array.prototype`, you cannot invoke array methods on them directly. You can invoke them indirectly using the `Function.call` method (see "Indirect Invocation" on page 120), however:

```
// An array-like object
var a = {"0":"a", "1":"b", "2":"c", length:3};
Array.prototype.join.call(a, "+") // => "a+b+c"
Array.prototype.map.call(a, function(x) {
    return x.toUpperCase();
})                                 // => ["A","B","C"]
// Make a true array copy of a n array-like object
Array.prototype.slice.call(a, 0)  // => ["a","b","c"]
```

Some browsers define generic array functions directly on the `Array` constructor. In browsers that support them, the examples above can be rewritten like this:

```
var a = {"0":"a", "1":"b", "2":"c", length:3};
Array.join(a, "+")
Array.slice(a, 0)
Array.map(a, function(x) { return x.toUpperCase(); })
```

Strings as Arrays

In ECMAScript 5 (and in many recent browser implementations—including IE8—prior to ECMAScript 5), strings behave like read-only arrays. Instead of accessing individual characters with the `charAt()` method, you can use square brackets:

```
var s = test;
s.charAt(0)    // => "t"
s[1]           // => "e"
```

The `typeof` operator still returns "string" for strings, of course, and the `Array.isArray()` method returns `false` if you pass it a string.

The primary benefit of indexable strings is simply that we can replace calls to **charAt()** with square brackets, which are more concise and readable. The fact that strings behave like arrays also means, however, that we can apply generic array methods to them. For example:

```
s = "Java"
Array.prototype.join.call(s, " ")    // => "J a v a"
Array.prototype.filter.call(s, function(x) {
        return x.match(/[^aeiou]/); // Match nonvowels
    }).join("")                      // => "Jv"
```

CHAPTER 7

Functions

A *function* is a block of JavaScript code that is defined once but may be executed, or *invoked*, any number of times. You may already be familiar with the concept of a function under a name such as *subroutine* or *procedure*. JavaScript functions are *parameterized*: a function definition may include a list of identifiers, known as *parameters*, that work as local variables for the body of the function. Function invocations provide values, or *arguments*, for the function's parameters. Functions often use their argument values to compute a *return value* that becomes the value of the function-invocation expression. In addition to the arguments, each invocation has another value—the *invocation context*—that is the value of the **this** keyword.

If a function is assigned to the property of an object, it is known as a *method* of that object. When a function is invoked *on* or *through* an object, that object is the invocation context or **this** value for the function. Functions designed to initialize a newly created object are called *constructors*. Constructors were described in "Creating Objects" on page 76 and will be covered again in Chapter 8.

In JavaScript, functions are objects, and they can be manipulated by programs. JavaScript can assign functions to variables and pass them to other functions, for example. Since functions are objects, you can set properties on them, and even invoke methods on them.

JavaScript function definitions can be nested within other functions, and they have access to any variables that are in scope where they are defined. This means that JavaScript functions are *closures*, and it enables important and powerful programming techniques.

Defining Functions

Functions are defined with the `function` keyword, which can be used in a function definition expression ("Function Definition" on page 26) or in a function declaration statement ("function" on page 54). In either form, function definitions begin with the keyword `function` followed by these components:

- An identifier that names the function. The name is a required part of function declaration statements: it is used as the name of a variable, and the newly defined function object is assigned to the variable. For function definition expressions, the name is optional: if present, the name refers to the function object only within the body of the function itself.

- A pair of parentheses around a comma-separated list of zero or more identifiers. These identifiers are the parameter names for the function, and they behave like local variables within the body of the function.

- A pair of curly braces with zero or more JavaScript statements inside. These statements are the body of the function: they are executed whenever the function is invoked.

Example 7-1 shows some function definitions using both statement and expression forms. Notice that a function defined as an expression is only useful if it is part of a larger expression, such as an assignment or invocation, that does something with the newly defined function.

Example 7-1. Defining JavaScript functions

```javascript
// Print the name and value of each property of o.
// Return undefined.
function printprops(o) {
    for(var p in o)
        console.log(p + ": " + o[p] + "\n");
}

// Compute distance between points (x1,y1) and (x2,y2).
function distance(x1, y1, x2, y2) {
    var dx = x2 - x1;
    var dy = y2 - y1;
    return Math.sqrt(dx*dx + dy*dy);
}

// A recursive function (one that calls itself) that
// computes factorials. Recall that x! is the product of
// x and all positive integers less than it.
function factorial(x) {
    if (x <= 1) return 1;
    return x * factorial(x-1);
}

// This expression defines a function that sqares its
// argument. Note that we assign it to a variable
var square = function(x) { return x*x; }

// Function expressions can include names,
// which is useful for recursion.
var f = function fact(x) {
    if (x <= 1) return 1;
    else return x*fact(x-1);
};

// Function expressions can also be used
// as arguments to other functions:
data.sort(function(a,b) { return a-b; });

// Function expressions are sometimes
// defined and then immediately invoked:
var tensquared = (function(x) {return x*x;}(10));
```

Note that the function name is optional for functions defined as expressions. A function declaration statement actually *declares* a variable and assigns a function object to it. A function definition expression, on the other hand, does not declare a variable. A name is allowed for functions, like the factorial function above, that need to refer to themselves. If a function definition expression includes a name, the local function scope for that function will include a binding of that name to the function object. In effect, the function name becomes a local variable within the function. Most functions defined as expressions do not need names, which makes their definition more compact. Function definition expressions are particularly well suited for functions that are used only once, as in the last two examples above.

As described in "function" on page 54, function declaration statements are "hoisted" to the top of the enclosing script or the enclosing function, so that functions declared in this way may be invoked from code that appears before they are defined. This is not true for functions defined as expressions, however: in order to invoke a function, you must be able to refer to it, and you can't refer to a function defined as an expression until it is assigned to a variable. So functions defined with expressions cannot be invoked before they are defined.

Notice that most, but not all, of the functions in Example 7-1 contain a return statement ("return" on page 66). The return statement causes the function to stop executing and to return the value of its expression (if any) to the caller. If the return statement does not have an associated expression, it returns the undefined value. If a function does not contain a return statement, it simply executes each statement in the function body and returns the undefined value to the caller.

Nested Functions

In JavaScript, functions may be nested within other functions. For example:

```
function hypotenuse(a, b) {
    function square(x) { return x*x; }
    return Math.sqrt(square(a) + square(b));
}
```

The interesting thing about nested functions is their variable scoping rules: they can access the parameters and variables of the function (or functions) they are nested within. In the code above, for example, the inner function square() can read and write the parameters a and b defined by the outer function hypotenuse(). These scope rules for nested functions are very important, and we'll consider them again in "Closures" on page 125.

As noted in "function" on page 54, function declaration statements are not true statements, and the ECMAScript specification only allows them as top-level statements. They can appear in global code, or within other functions, but they cannot appear inside of loops, conditionals, or try/catch/finally or with statements. Note that this restriction applies only to functions declared as statements. Function definition expressions may appear anywhere in your JavaScript code.

Invoking Functions

The JavaScript code that makes up the body of a function is not executed when the function is defined but when it is invoked. JavaScript functions can be invoked in four ways:

- as functions,
- as methods,
- as constructors, and
- indirectly through their call() and apply() methods.

Function Invocation

Functions are invoked as functions or as methods with an invocation expression ("Invocation" on page 27). An invocation expression consists of a function expression that evaluates to a function object followed by an open parenthesis, a comma-separated list of zero or more argument expressions, and a close parenthesis. If the function expression is a property-access expression—if the function is the property of an object or an element of an array—then it is a method invocation expression. That case will be explained below. The following code includes a number of regular function invocation expressions:

```
printprops({x:1});
var total = distance(0,0,2,1) + distance(2,1,3,5);
var probability = factorial(5)/factorial(13);
```

In an invocation, each argument expression (the ones between the parentheses) is evaluated, and the resulting values become the arguments to the function. These values are assigned to the parameters named in the function definition. In the body of the function, a reference to a parameter evaluates to the corresponding argument value.

For regular function invocation, the return value of the function becomes the value of the invocation expression. If the function returns because the interpreter reaches the end, the return value is undefined. If the function returns because the interpreter executes a return, the return value is the value of the expression that follows the return or undefined if the return statement has no value.

For function invocation in ECMAScript 3 and nonstrict ECMAScript 5, the invocation context (the this value) is the global object. In strict mode, however, the invocation context is undefined.

Functions written to be invoked as functions do not typically use the this keyword at all. It can be used, however, to determine whether strict mode is in effect:

```
// Define and invoke a function to determine
// if we're in strict mode.
var strict = (function() { return !this; }());
```

Method Invocation

A *method* is nothing more than a JavaScript function that is stored in a property of an object. If you have a function f and an object o, you can define a method named m of o with the following line:

```
o.m = f;
```

Having defined the method m() of the object o, invoke it like this:

```
o.m();
```

Or, if m() expects two arguments, you might invoke it like this:

```
o.m(x, y);
```

The code above is an invocation expression: it includes a function expression o.m and two argument expressions, x and y. The function expression is itself a property access expression ("Property Access" on page 26), and this means that the function is invoked as a method rather than as a regular function.

The arguments and return value of a method invocation are handled exactly as described above for regular function invocation. Method invocations differ from function invocations in one important way, however: the invocation context. Property access expressions consist of two parts: an object (in this case o) and a property name (m). In a method invocation expression like this, the object o becomes the invocation context, and the function body can refer to that object by using the keyword this. Here is a concrete example:

```
var calculator = {  // An object literal
    operand1: 1,
    operand2: 1,
    add: function() {
        // The this keyword refers to this object.
        this.result = this.operand1 + this.operand2;
    }
};
calculator.add(); // A method invocation to compute 1+1.
calculator.result // => 2
```

Most method invocations use the dot notation for property access, but property access expressions that use square brackets also cause method invocation. The following are both method invocations, for example:

```
o["m"](x,y); // Another way to write o.m(x,y).
a = [function(x) { return x+1 }];
a[0](z)      // Also a method invocation
```

Method invocations may also involve more complex property access expressions:

```
// Invoke toUpperCase() method on customer.surname
customer.surname.toUpperCase();
// Invoke method m() on return value of f()
f().m();
```

Note that this is a keyword, not a variable or property name. JavaScript syntax does not allow you to assign a value to this.

Unlike variables, the this keyword does not have a scope, and nested functions do not inherit the this value of the containing function. If a nested function is invoked as a method, its this value is the object it was invoked on. If a nested function is invoked as a function, its this value will be either the global object (nonstrict mode) or undefined (strict mode). It is a common mistake to assume that a nested function invoked as a function can use this to obtain the invocation context of the outer function. If you want to access the this value of the outer function, you need to store that value into a variable that is in scope for the inner function. It is common to use the variable self for this purpose. For example:

```
var o = {              // An object o.
    m: function() {    // Method m of the object.
        var self = this;  // Save the this value
        console.log(this === o); // Prints "true"
        f();              // Now call nested function

        function f() {
            console.log(this === o); // prints "false"
            console.log(self === o); // prints "true"
        }
    }
};
o.m(); // Invoke the method m on the object o.
```

Constructor Invocation

If a function or method invocation is preceded by the keyword new, then it is a constructor invocation. (Constructor invocations were introduced in "Initializers" on page 24 and

"Creating Objects with new" on page 76, and constructors will be covered in more detail in Chapter 8.) Constructor invocations differ from regular function and method invocations in their handling of arguments, invocation context, and return value.

If a constructor invocation includes an argument list in parentheses, those argument expressions are evaluated and passed to the function in the same way they would be for function and method invocations. But if a constructor has no parameters, then JavaScript constructor invocation syntax allows the argument list and parentheses to be omitted entirely. You can always omit a pair of empty parentheses in a constructor invocation and the following two lines, for example, are equivalent:

```
var o = new Object();
var o = new Object;
```

A constructor invocation creates a new, empty object that inherits from the **prototype** property of the constructor. Constructor functions are intended to initialize objects and this newly created object is used as the invocation context, so the constructor function can refer to it with the **this** keyword. Note that the new object is used as the invocation context even if the constructor invocation looks like a method invocation. That is, in the expression new `o.m()`, `o` is not used as the invocation context.

Constructor functions do not normally use the **return** keyword. They typically initialize the new object and then return implicitly when they reach the end of their body. In this case, the new object is the value of the constructor invocation expression. If, however, a constructor explicitly used the **return** statement to return an object, then that object becomes the value of the invocation expression. If the constructor uses **return** with no value, or if it returns a primitive value, that return value is ignored and the new object is used as the value of the invocation.

Indirect Invocation

JavaScript functions are objects and like all JavaScript objects, they have methods. Two of these methods, `call()` and `apply()`, invoke the function indirectly. The first argument to both `call()` and `apply()` is the object on which the function is to be invoked; this argument is the invocation context and becomes the value of the `this` keyword within the body of the function. To invoke the function `f()` as a method of the object `o` (passing no arguments), you could use either `call()` or `apply()`:

```
f.call(o);
f.apply(o);
```

Either of the lines of code above are similar to the following (which assume that `o` does not already have a property named `m`):

```
o.m = f;       // Make f a temporary method of o.
o.m();         // Invoke it, passing no arguments.
delete o.m;    // Remove the temporary method.
```

In ECMAScript 5 strict mode, the first argument to `call()` or `apply()` becomes the value of `this`, even if it is a primitive value or `null` or `undefined`. In ECMAScript 3 and nonstrict mode, a value of `null` or `undefined` is replaced with the global object and a primitive value is replaced with the corresponding wrapper object.

Any arguments to `call()` after the first invocation context argument are the values that are passed to the function that is invoked. For example, to pass two numbers to the function `f()` and invoke it as if it were a method of the object `o`, you could use code like this:

```
f.call(o, 1, 2);
```

The `apply()` method is like the `call()` method, except that the arguments to be passed to the function are specified as an array:

```
f.apply(o, [1,2]);
```

If a function is defined to accept an arbitrary number of arguments, the `apply()` method allows you to invoke that function on the contents of an array of arbitrary length. For example, to find the largest number in an array of numbers, you could use the `apply()` method to pass the elements of the array to the `Math.max()` function:

```
var biggest = Math.max.apply(Math, array_of_numbers);
```

Note that `apply()` works with array-like objects as well as true arrays. In particular, you can invoke a function with the same arguments as the current function by passing the `arguments` array (see "Variable-Length Argument Lists: The Arguments Object" on page 122) directly to `apply()`. The following code demonstrates:

```
// Replace the method named m of the object o with a
// version that logs messages before and after invoking
// the original method.
function trace(o, m) {
    var original = o[m];  // Remember original method.
    o[m] = function() {   // Now define the new method.
        console.log(new Date(), "Entering:", m); // Log
        // Invoke the original method
        var result = original.apply(this, arguments);
        console.log(new Date(), "Exiting:", m);  // Log
        // Return the result of the original method
        return result;
    };
}
```

This `trace()` function is passed an object and a method name. It replaces the specified method with a new method that "wraps" additional functionality around the original method. This kind of dynamic alteration of existing methods is sometimes called "monkey-patching."

Function Arguments and Parameters

JavaScript function definitions do not specify an expected type for the function parameters, and function invocations do not do any type checking on the argument values you pass. In fact,

JavaScript function invocations do not even check the number of arguments being passed. The subsections that follow describe what happens when a function is invoked with fewer arguments than declared parameters or with more arguments than declared parameters.

Optional Parameters

When a function is invoked with fewer arguments than declared parameters, the additional parameters are set to the undefined value. It is often useful to write functions so that some arguments are optional and may be omitted when the function is invoked. To do this, you must be able to assign a reasonable default value to parameters that are omitted. Here is an example:

```
// Append the names of the enumerable properties of
// object o to the array a, and return a.  If a is
// omitted, create and return a new array.
function names(o, /* optional */ a) {
    if (a === undefined)  // If a was not specified
        a = [];           // use a new array.
    for(var property in o) a.push(property);
    return a;
}

// This function can be invoked with 1 or 2 arguments:
var a = names(o); // Get o's properties in a new array
names(p,a);       // Append p's properties to that array.
```

Instead of using an if statement in the first line of this function, you could use the || operator ("Logical Expressions" on page 39) in this idiomatic way:

```
a = a || [];
```

Variable-Length Argument Lists: The Arguments Object

When a function is invoked with more argument values than there are parameter names, there is no way to directly refer to the unnamed values. The Arguments object provides a solution to this problem. Within the body of a function, the identifier arguments refers to the Arguments object for that invocation. The Arguments object is an array-like object (see "Array-Like Objects" on page 107) that allows the argument values passed to the function to be retrieved by number, rather than by name.

Suppose you define a function f that expects to be passed one argument, x. If you invoke this function with two arguments, the first argument is accessible within the function by the parameter name x or as arguments[0]. The second argument is accessible only as arguments[1]. Furthermore, arguments has a length property that specifies the number of elements it contains. Thus, within the body of the function f, invoked with two arguments, arguments.length has the value 2.

One important use of the Arguments object is to write functions that operate on any number of arguments. The following function accepts any number of numeric arguments and returns the value of the largest argument it is passed (see also the built-in function Math.max(), which behaves the same way):

```
function max(/* ... */) {
    var max = Number.NEGATIVE_INFINITY;
    // Look for and remember the largest argument
    for(var i = 0; i < arguments.length; i++)
        if (arguments[i] > max) max = arguments[i];
    // Return the biggest
    return max;
}
var largest = max(10, 100, 2, 4, 10000, 6);  // => 10000
```

Functions like this one that can accept any number of arguments are called *variadic functions*, *variable arity functions*, or *varargs functions*. This book uses the most colloquial term, *varargs*, which dates to the early days of the C programming language.

Note that varargs functions need not allow invocations with zero arguments. It is perfectly reasonable to use the arguments[] object to write functions that expect some fixed number of named and required arguments followed by an arbitrary number of unnamed optional arguments.

Functions as Namespaces

Recall from "Variable Declaration" on page 19 that JavaScript has function scope: variables declared within a function are visible throughout the function (including within nested functions) but do not exist outside of the function. Variables declared outside of a function are global variables and are visible throughout your JavaScript program. JavaScript does not define any way to declare variables that are hidden within a single block of code, and for this reason, it is sometimes useful to define a function simply to act as a temporary namespace in which you can define variables without polluting the global namespace.

Suppose, for example, you have a module of JavaScript code that you want to use in a number of different JavaScript programs (or, for client-side JavaScript, on a number of different web pages). Assume that this code, like most code, defines variables to store the intermediate results of its computation. The problem is that since this module will be used in many different programs, you don't know whether the variables it creates will conflict with variables used by the programs that import it. The solution, of course, is to put the code into a function and then invoke the function. This way, variables that would have been global become local to the function:

```
function mymodule() {
    // Module code goes here.
    // Any variables used by the module are local to this
    // function and do not clutter the global namespace.
}
mymodule();  // But don't forget to invoke the function!
```

This code defines only a single global variable: the function name "mymodule." If defining even a single property is too much, you can define and invoke an anonymous function in a single expression:

```
(function() {  // mymodule as an unnamed expression
    // Module code goes here.
}());          // end the function and invoke it.
```

This technique of defining and invoking a function in a single expression is used frequently enough that it has become idiomatic. Note the use of parentheses in the code above. The open parenthesis before function is required because without it, the JavaScript interpreter tries to parse the function keyword as a function declaration statement. With the parenthesis, the interpreter correctly recognizes this as a function definition expression. It is idiomatic to use the parentheses, even when they are not required, around a function that is to be invoked immediately after being defined.

Closures

Like most modern programming languages, JavaScript uses *lexical scoping*. This means that functions are executed using the variable scope that was in effect when they were defined, not the variable scope that is in effect when they are invoked. This combination of a function object and the scope (a set of variable bindings) in which it was defined is known as a *closure*, and closures become interesting in JavaScript when nested functions are involved. There are a number of powerful programming techniques that involve this kind of nested function closures, and their use has become common in modern JavaScript programming. Closures can be confusing when you first encounter them, but it is important that you understand them well enough to use them comfortably.

The first step to understanding closures is to review the lexical scoping rules for nested functions. Consider the following code:

```
var scope = "global scope";        // A global variable
function checkscope() {
    var scope = "local scope";     // A local variable
    function f() { return scope; }
    return f();
}
checkscope()      // => "local scope"
```

The `checkscope()` function declares a local variable and then defines and invokes a function that returns the value of that variable. It should be clear to you why the call to `check scope()` returns "local scope." Now let's change the code just slightly. Can you tell what this code will return?

```
var scope = "global scope";        // A global variable
function checkscope() {
    var scope = "local scope";     // A local variable
    function f() { return scope; }
    return f;
}
checkscope()()   // What does this return?
```

In this code, a pair of parentheses has moved from inside `check scope()` to outside of it. Instead of invoking the nested function and returning its result, `checkscope()` now just returns the nested function object itself. What happens when we invoke that nested function (with the second pair of parentheses in the last line of code) outside of the function in which it was defined?

Remember the fundamental rule of lexical scoping: JavaScript functions are executed using the scope chain that was in effect when they were defined. The nested function `f()` was defined under a scope chain in which the variable `scope` was bound to the value "local scope." That binding is still in effect when `f` is executed, wherever it is executed from. So the last line of code above returns "local scope," not "global scope." This, in a nutshell, is the surprising and powerful nature of closures: they capture the local variable (and parameter) bindings of the outer function within which they are defined.

Closures capture the local variables of a single function invocation and can use those variables as private state. The following code uses a closure in this way:

```
var uniqueInteger = (function() { // Define and invoke
    var counter = 0;  // Private state of function below
    return function() { return counter++; };
}());
```

In order to understand this code, you have to read it carefully. At first glance, the first line of code looks like it is assigning a function to the variable `uniqueInteger`. In fact, the code is defining and invoking (as hinted by the open parenthesis on the first line) a function, so it is the return value of the function that is being assigned to `uniqueInteger`. Now, if we study the body of the function, we see that its return value is another function. It is this nested function object that gets assigned to `uniqueInteger`. The nested function has access to the variables in scope, and can use the `counter` variable defined in the outer function. Once that outer function returns, no other code can see the `counter` variable: the inner function has exclusive access to it. Each invocation of `uniqueInteger()` will return a new integer, and there is no way for JavaScript code to alter the internal `counter`.

Private variables like `counter` need not be exclusive to a single function: it is perfectly possible for two or more nested functions to be defined within the same outer function and share access to the same private variables. Consider the following code:

```
function counter() {
    var n = 0;
    return {
        count: function() { return n++; },
        reset: function() { n = 0; }
    };
}

var c = counter(),     // Create two counters
    d = counter();
c.count()  // => 0
d.count()  // => 0: they count independently
c.reset()  // reset() and count() methods share state
c.count()  // => 0: because we reset c
d.count()  // => 1: d was not reset
```

The `counter()` function returns a "counter" object. This object has two methods: `count()` returns the next integer, and `reset()` resets the internal state. The first thing to understand is that the two methods share access to the private variable n. The second thing to understand is that each invocation of `counter()` creates a new scope chain and a new private variable.

So if you call **counter()** twice, you get two counter objects with different private variables. Calling **count()** or **reset()** on one counter object has no effect on the other.

In the example above, two functions are defined in the same scope chain and share access to the same private variable or variables. This is an important technique, but it is just as important to recognize when closures inadvertently share access to a variable that they should not share. Consider the following code:

```
// This function returns a function that always returns v
function constant(v) { return function() { return v; }; }

// Create an array of constant functions:
var funcs = [];
for(var i = 0; i < 10; i++) funcs[i] = constant(i);

// The function at array element 5 returns the value 5.
funcs[5]()    // => 5
```

When working with code like this that creates multiple closures using a loop, it is a common error to try to move the loop within the function that defines the closures. Think about the following code, for example:

```
// Return an array of functions that return 0-9
function constfuncs() {
    var funcs = [];
    for(var i = 0; i < 10; i++)
        funcs[i] = function() { return i; };
    return funcs;
}

var funcs = constfuncs();
funcs[5]()    // What does this return?
```

The code above creates 10 closures, and stores them in an array. The closures are all defined within the same invocation of the function, so they share access to the variable i. When con stfuncs() returns, the value of the variable i is 10, and all 10 closures share this value. Therefore, all the functions in the returned array of functions return the same value, which is not what we wanted at all. It is important to remember that the scope chain associated with a closure is "live." Nested functions do not make private copies of the scope or make static snapshots of the variable bindings.

Another thing to remember when writing closures is that `this` is a JavaScript keyword, not a variable. As discussed earlier, every function invocation has a `this` value, and a closure cannot access the `this` value of its outer function unless the outer function has saved that value into a variable:

```
var self = this; // for use by nested funcs.
```

The `arguments` binding is similar. This is not a language keyword, but it is automatically declared for every function invocation. Since a closure has its own binding for `arguments`, it cannot access the outer function's arguments array unless the outer function has saved that array into a variable by a different name:

```
var outerArguments = arguments; // For nested funcs
```

Function Properties, Methods, and Constructor

We've seen that functions are values in JavaScript programs. The `typeof` operator returns the string "function" when applied to a function, but functions are really a specialized kind of JavaScript object. Since functions are objects, they can have properties and methods, just like any other object. There is even a `Function()` constructor to create new function objects. The `call()` and `apply()` methods of function objects were covered in "Indirect Invocation" on page 120, and the subsections that follow document the remaining function properties and methods and the `Function()` constructor.

The length Property

Within the body of a function, `arguments.length` specifies the number of arguments that were passed to the function. The `length` property of a function itself, however, has a different meaning. This read-only property returns the *arity* of the function—the number of parameters it declares in its parameter list, which is usually the number of arguments that the function expects.

The prototype Property

Every function has a `prototype` property that refers to an object known as the *prototype object*. Every function has a different prototype object. When a function is used as a constructor, the newly created object inherits properties from the prototype object. Prototypes and the `prototype` property were discussed in "Prototypes" on page 77 and will be covered again in Chapter 8.

The bind() Method

The `bind()` method was added in ECMAScript 5, but it is easy to simulate in ECMAScript 3. As its name implies, the primary purpose of `bind()` is to bind a function to an object. When you invoke the `bind()` method on a function f and pass an object o, the method returns a new function. Invoking the new function (as a function) invokes the original function f as a method of o. Any arguments you pass to the new function are passed to the original function. For example:

```
// This function needs to be bound
function f(y) { return this.x + y; }
var o = { x : 1 };  // An object we'll bind to
var g = f.bind(o);  // Calling g(x) invokes o.f(x)
g(2)                // => 3
```

It is easy to accomplish this kind of binding with code like the following:

```
// Return a function that invokes f as a method of o,
// passing all its arguments.
function bind(f, o) {
    // Use the bind method, if there is one
    if (f.bind) return f.bind(o);
    else return function() {
        // Otherwise, bind it like this
```

```
        return f.apply(o, arguments);
    };
}
```

The ECMAScript 5 `bind()` method does more than just bind a function to an object. It also performs partial application: any arguments you pass to `bind()` after the first are bound along with the `this` value. Partial application is a common technique in functional programming and is sometimes called *currying*. Here is an example of the `bind()` method used for partial application:

```
var sum = function(x,y) { return x + y };
// Create a new function like sum, but with the this
// value bound to null and the 1st argument bound to 1.
// This new function expects just one arg.
var succ = sum.bind(null, 1);
succ(2) // => 3: x is bound to 1, and we pass 2 for y.
```

The toString() Method

Like all JavaScript objects, functions have a `toString()` method. The ECMAScript spec requires this method to return a string that follows the syntax of the function declaration statement. In practice, most (but not all) implementations of this `toString()` method return the complete source code for the function. Built-in functions typically return a string that includes something like "[native code]" as the function body.

The Function() Constructor

Functions are usually defined using the `function` keyword, either in the form of a function definition statement or a function literal expression. But functions can also be defined with the `Function()` constructor. For example:

```
var f = new Function("x", "y", "return x*y;");
```

This line of code creates a new function that is more or less equivalent to a function defined with the familiar syntax:

```
var f = function(x, y) { return x*y; }
```

The Function() constructor expects any number of string arguments. The last argument is the text of the function body; it can contain arbitrary JavaScript statements, separated from each other by semicolons. All other arguments to the constructor are strings that specify the parameter names for the function. If you are defining a function that takes no arguments, you simply pass a single string—the function body—to the constructor.

A very important point about the Function() constructor is that the functions it creates do not use lexical scoping; instead, they are always compiled as if they were top-level functions: they can access global variables, but not any local variables.

CHAPTER 8

Classes

JavaScript objects were covered in Chapter 5. That chapter treated each object as a unique set of properties, different from every other object. It is often useful, however, to define a *class* of objects that share certain properties. Members, or *instances*, of the class have their own properties to hold or define their state, but they also have properties (typically methods) that define their behavior. This behavior is defined by the class and is shared by all instances. Imagine a class named Complex to represent and perform arithmetic on complex numbers, for example. A Complex instance would have properties to hold the real and imaginary parts (state) of the complex number. And the Complex class would define methods to perform addition and multiplication (behavior) of those numbers.

In JavaScript, classes are based on JavaScript's prototype-based inheritance mechanism. If two objects inherit properties from the same prototype object, then we say that they are instances of the same class. JavaScript prototypes and inheritance were covered in "Prototypes" on page 77 and "Property Inheritance" on page 80, and you must be familiar with the material in those sections to understand this chapter. This chapter covers prototypes in "Classes and Prototypes" on page 134.

If two objects inherit from the same prototype, this typically (but not necessarily) means that they were created and initialized by the same constructor function. Constructors have been covered in "Initializers" on page 24, "Creating Objects with new" on page 76, and "Constructor Invocation" on page 118, and this chapter has more in "Classes and Constructors" on page 136.

If you're familiar with strongly-typed object-oriented programming languages like Java or C++, you'll notice that JavaScript classes are quite different from classes in those languages. There are some syntactic similarities, and you can emulate many features of "classical" classes in JavaScript, but it is best to understand up front that JavaScript's classes and prototype-based inheritance mechanism are substantially different from the classes and class-based inheritance mechanism of Java and similar languages. "Java-Style Classes in Java-Script" on page 141 demonstrates classical classes in Java-Script. One of the important features of JavaScript classes is that they are dynamically extendable. "Augmenting Classes" on page 146 explains how to do this.

Classes and Prototypes

In JavaScript, a class is a set of objects that inherit properties from the same prototype object. The prototype object, therefore, is the central feature of a class. In Example 5-1 we defined an inherit() function that returns a newly created object that inherits from a specified prototype object. In this chapter we'll use the built-in ES5 function Object.create() instead of the more portable inherit() utility function. If we define a prototype object, and then use Object.create() to create objects that inherit from it, we have defined a JavaScript class. Usually, the instances of a class require further initialization, and it is common to define a function that creates and initializes the new object. Example 8-1 demonstrates this: it defines a prototype object for a class that represents a range of values and also defines a "factory" function that creates and initializes a new instance of the class.

Example 8-1. A simple JavaScript class

```javascript
// range.js: A class representing a range of values.

// This is a factory function that returns a new range object.
function range(from, to) {
    // Use Object.create() to create an object that inherits
    // from the prototype object defined below. The prototype
    // is stored as a property of this function, and defines
    // the shared methods (behavior) for all range objects.
    var r = Object.create(range.methods);

    // Save the start and end points (state) of the object.
    // They are noninherited properties unique to this object.
    r.from = from;
    r.to = to;

    // Finally return the new object
    return r;
}

// This prototype object defines methods inherited by all
// range objects.
range.methods = {
    // Return true if x is in the range, false otherwise
    includes: function(x) {
        return this.from <= x && x <= this.to;
    },
    // Invoke f once for each integer in the range.
    // This method works only for numeric ranges.
    foreach: function(f) {
        for(var x=Math.ceil(this.from); x <= this.to; x++)
            f(x);
    },
    // Return a string representation of the range
    toString: function() {
        return "(" + this.from + "..." + this.to + ")";
    }
};

// Here are example uses of a range object.
var r = range(1,3);        // Create a range object
r.includes(2);             // => true: 2 is in the range
r.foreach(console.log);    // Prints 1 2 3
console.log(r);            // Prints (1...3)
```

There are a few things worth noting in the code of Example 8-1. This code defines a factory function `range()` for creating new range objects. Notice that we use a property of this `range()` function, `range.methods`, as a convenient place to store the prototype object that defines the class. There is nothing special or idiomatic about putting the prototype object here. Second, notice that the `range()` function defines `from` and `to` properties on each range object. These are the unshared, noninherited properties that define the unique state of each individual range object. Finally, notice that the shared, inherited methods defined in `range.methods` all use these `from` and `to` properties, and in order to refer to them, they use the `this` keyword to refer to the object through which they were invoked. This use of `this` is a fundamental characteristic of the methods of any class.

Classes and Constructors

Example 8-1 demonstrates one way to define a JavaScript class. It is not the idiomatic way to do so, however, because it did not define a *constructor*. A constructor is a function designed for the initialization of newly created objects. Constructors are invoked using the `new` keyword as described in "Constructor Invocation" on page 118. Constructor invocations using `new` automatically create the new object, so the constructor itself only needs to initialize the state of that new object. The critical feature of constructor invocations is that the `prototype` property of the constructor function is used as the prototype of the new object. This means that all objects created with the same constructor inherit from the same object and are therefore members of the same class. Example 8-2 shows how we could alter the Range class of Example 8-1 to use a constructor function instead of a factory function:

Example 8-2. A Range class using a constructor

```
// range2.js: Another class representing a range of values.

// This is a constructor function that initializes new
```

```
// Range objects. Note that it does not create or return
// the object. It just initializes this.
function Range(from, to) {
    // Store the start and end points (state) of this new
    // range object. These are noninherited properties that
    // are unique to this object.
    this.from = from;
    this.to = to;
}

// All Range objects inherit from this object.
// Note that the property name must be "prototype".
Range.prototype = {
    // Return true if x is in the range, false otherwise
    includes: function(x) {
        return this.from <= x && x <= this.to;
    },
    // Invoke f once for each integer in the range.
    foreach: function(f) {
        for(var x=Math.ceil(this.from); x <= this.to; x++)
            f(x);
    },
    // Return a string representation of the range
    toString: function() {
        return "(" + this.from + "..." + this.to + ")";
    }
};

// Here are example uses of a range object
var r = new Range(1,3);    // Create a range object
r.includes(2);             // => true: 2 is in the range
r.foreach(console.log);    // Prints 1 2 3
console.log(r);            // Prints (1...3)
```

It is worth comparing Example 8-1 and Example 8-2 carefully and noting the differences between these two techniques for defining classes. First, notice that we renamed the **range()** factory function to **Range()** when we converted it to a constructor. This is a very common coding convention: constructor functions define, in a sense, classes, and classes have names that begin with capital letters. Regular functions and methods have names that begin with lowercase letters.

Next, notice that the **Range()** constructor is invoked (at the end of the example) with the **new** keyword while the **range()** factory function was invoked without it. Example 8-1 uses regular function invocation ("Function Invocation" on page 115) to create the new object and Example 8-2 uses constructor invocation ("Constructor Invocation" on page 118). Because the `Range()` constructor is invoked with `new`, it does not have to call `Object.create()` or take any action to create a new object. The new object is automatically created before the constructor is called, and it is accessible as the `this` value. The `Range()` constructor merely has to initialize `this`. Constructors do not even have to return the newly created object. Constructor invocation automatically creates a new object, invokes the constructor as a method of that object, and returns the new object.

Another critical difference between Example 8-1 and Example 8-2 is the way the prototype object is named. In the first example, the prototype was `range.methods`. This was a convenient and descriptive name, but arbitrary. In the second example, the prototype is `Range.prototype`, and this name is mandatory. An invocation of the `Range()` constructor automatically uses `Range.prototype` as the prototype of the new Range object.

Finally, also note the things that do not change between Example 8-1 and Example 8-2: the range methods are defined and invoked in the same way for both classes.

Constructors and Class Identity

As we've seen, the prototype object is fundamental to the identity of a class: two objects are instances of the same class if and only if they inherit from the same prototype object. The constructor function that initializes the state of a new object is not fundamental: two constructor functions may have `prototype` properties that point to the same prototype object. Then both constructors can be used to create instances of the same class.

Even though constructors are not as fundamental as prototypes, the constructor serves as the public face of a class. Most obviously, the name of the constructor function is usually adopted as the name of the class. We say, for example, that the

`Range()` constructor creates Range objects. More fundamentally, however, constructors are used with the `instanceof` operator when testing objects for membership in a class. If we have an object `r` and want to know if it is a Range object, we can write:

```
// true if r inherits from Range.prototype
r instanceof Range
```

The `instanceof` operator does not actually check whether `r` was initialized by the `Range` constructor. It checks whether it inherits from `Range.prototype`. Nevertheless, the `instanceof` syntax reinforces the use of constructors as the public identity of a class. We'll see the `instanceof` operator again later in this chapter.

The constructor Property

In Example 8-2 we set `Range.prototype` to a new object that contained the methods for our class. Although it was convenient to express those methods as properties of a single object literal, it was not actually necessary to create a new object. Any JavaScript function can be used as a constructor, and constructor invocations need a **prototype** property. Therefore, every JavaScript function automatically has a **prototype** property. The value of this property is an object that has a single nonenumerable **constructor** property. The value of the constructor property is the function object:

```
// F.prototype.constructor === F for any function F.
var F = function() {};  // A function object.
var p = F.prototype;    // Its prototype object.
var c = p.constructor;  // The prototype's function
c === F                 // => true:
```

The existence of this predefined prototype object with its **constructor** property means that objects typically inherit a **constructor** property that refers to their constructor. Since constructors serve as the public identity of a class, this constructor property gives the class of an object:

```
var o = new F();    // Create an object o of class F
o.constructor === F // => true
```

Figure 8-1 illustrates this relationship between the constructor function, its prototype object, the back reference from the prototype to the constructor, and the instances created with the constructor.

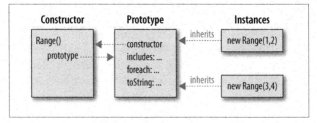

Figure 8-1. A constructor function, its prototype, and instances

Notice that Figure 8-1 uses our `Range()` constructor as an example. In fact, however, the Range class defined in Example 8-2 overwrites the predefined `Range.prototype` object with an object of its own. And the new prototype object it defines does not have a `constructor` property. So instances of the Range class, as defined, do not have a `constructor` property. We can remedy this problem by explicitly adding a constructor to the prototype:

```
Range.prototype = {
    constructor: Range, // Explicitly set the constructor
    includes: function(x) {
        return this.from <= x && x <= this.to;
    },
    // etc...
};
```

Another common technique is to use the predefined prototype object with its `constructor` property, and add methods to it one at a time:

```
// Extend the predefined Range.prototype object so we
// don't overwrite Range.prototype.constructor.
Range.prototype.includes = function(x) {
    return this.from<=x && x<=this.to;
```

```
};
Range.prototype.foreach = function(f) {
    for(var x=Math.ceil(this.from); x <= this.to; x++)
        f(x);
};
Range.prototype.toString = function() {
    return "(" + this.from + "..." + this.to + ")";
};
```

Java-Style Classes in JavaScript

If you have programmed in Java or a similar strongly-typed object-oriented language, you may be accustomed to thinking about four kinds of class *members*:

Instance fields

These are the per-instance properties or variables that hold the state of individual objects.

Instance methods

These are methods that are shared by all instances of the class that are invoked through individual instances.

Class fields

These are properties or variables associated with the class rather than the instances of the class.

Class methods

These are methods that are associated with the class rather than with instances.

One way JavaScript differs from Java is that its functions are values, and there is no hard distinction between methods and fields. If the value of a property is a function, that property defines a method; otherwise, it is just an ordinary property or "field." Despite this difference, we can simulate each of Java's four categories of class members in JavaScript. In JavaScript, there are three different objects involved in any class definition (see Figure 8-1), and the properties of these three objects act like different kinds of class members:

Constructor object

As we've noted, the constructor function (an object) defines a name for a JavaScript class. Properties you add to this constructor object serve as class fields and class methods.

Prototype object

The properties of this object are inherited by all instances of the class, and properties whose values are functions behave like instance methods of the class.

Instance object

Each instance of a class is an object in its own right, and properties defined directly on an instance are not shared by any other instances. Nonfunction properties defined on instances behave as the instance fields of the class.

We can reduce the process of class definition in JavaScript to a three-step algorithm. First, write a constructor function that sets instance properties on new objects. Second, define instance methods on the **prototype** object of the constructor. Third, define class fields and class methods on the constructor itself. We can even implement this algorithm as a simple **defineClass()** function:

```
// A simple function for defining simple classes
function defineClass(constructor, // Initialization
                     methods,     // Instance methods
                     statics)     // Class properties
{
    if (methods) {
        // Copy methods to the prototype
        for(var m in methods)
            constructor.prototype[m] = methods[m];
    }
    if (statics) {
        // Copy static properties to the constructor
        for(var s in statics)
            constructor[s] = statics[s];
    }

    return constructor;
}
```

```
// This is a simple variant of our Range class
var SimpleRange =
    defineClass(
        function(f,t) { this.f = f; this.t = t; },
        {
            includes: function(x) {
                return this.f <= x && x <= this.t;
            },
            toString: function() {
                return this.f + "..." + this.t;
            }
        },
        {
            upto: function(t) {
                return new SimpleRange(0, t);
            }
        }
    );
```

Immutable Classes

"Property Attributes" on page 87 demonstrated the ECMA-Script 5 `Object.defineProperties()` method for defining read-only and nonenumerable properties, and also explained that property descriptors can also be passed to `Object.create`. We can use these ES5 features to define classes whose instances are immutable. Example 8-3 is an immutable version of our Range class with instance methods that are nonenumerable, like the methods of built-in classes. Finally, as an interesting trick, Example 8-3 has a constructor function that works as a factory function when invoked without the **new** keyword.

Example 8-3. An immutable class with nonenumerable methods

```
// This function works with or without 'new':
// it is a constructor and factory function.
function Range(from,to) {
    // These are descriptors for the read-only properties.
    var props = {
        from: { value:from, enumerable:true },
        to: { value:to, enumerable:true }
    };
```

```
    if (this instanceof Range)  // Invoked as a constructor
        Object.defineProperties(this, props);
    else                        // Invoked as a factory
        return Object.create(Range.prototype, props);
}

// Now set up the prototype with nonenumerable properties
Object.defineProperties(Range.prototype, {
    includes: {
        value: function(x) {
            return this.from <= x && x <= this.to;
        },
        writable: true, configurable: true
    },
    foreach: {
        value: function(f) {
            for(var x=Math.ceil(this.from); x<=this.to; x++)
                f(x);
        },
        writable: true, configurable: true
    },
    toString: {
        value: function() {
            return "(" + this.from + "..." + this.to + ")";
        },
        writable: true, configurable: true
    }
});
```

Subclasses

In object-oriented programming, a class B can *extend* or *subclass* another class A. We say that A is the *superclass* and B is the *subclass*. Instances of B inherit all the instance methods of A. The class B can define its own instance methods, some of which may *override* methods of the same name defined by class A.

The key to creating subclasses in JavaScript is proper initialization of the prototype object. If an object O is an instance of a class B and B is a subclass of A, then O must also inherit properties from A. We arrange this by ensuring that the prototype object of B inherits from the prototype object of A. Using

`Object.create()` (we could also use the `inherit()` function from Example 5-1), we write:

```
// Subclass B inherits from superclass A
B.prototype = Object.create(A.prototype);
// But override the inherited constructor prop.
B.prototype.constructor = B;
```

The two lines of code above are critical to creating subclasses in JavaScript. Without them, the prototype object will be an ordinary object—an object that inherits from `Object.proto type`—and this means that your class will be a subclass of Object like all classes are. It is straightforward to add these two lines to the `defineClass()` function above to transform it into `defineSubclass()`.

Example 8-4 defines a DateRange class as a subclass of Range. Date objects in JavaScript can be compared with < and >, so DateRange inherits the `includes()` and `toString()` methods. But it overrides the `foreach()` method to enumerate by days within the range. Note how the `DateRange.prototype` is set up, and also notice that the `DateRange()` constructor invokes its superclass constructor (using the `call()` method) to initialize the new object.

Example 8-4. A Range subclass

```
// A subclass of our Range class. It inherits the includes()
// and toString() methods, and overrides the foreach method
// to make it work with dates.
function DateRange(from, to) {
    // Use the superclass constructor to initialize
    Range.call(this, from, to);
}

// These two lines are key to subclassing. The subclass
// prototype must inherit from the superclass prototype.
DateRange.prototype = Object.create(Range.prototype);
DateRange.prototype.constructor = DateRange;

// This "static" field of the subclass holds the
// number of milliseconds in one day.
DateRange.DAY = 1000*60*60*24;
```

```
// Invoke f once for each day in the range
DateRange.prototype.foreach = function(f) {
    var d = this.from;
    while(d < this.to) {
        f(d);
        d = new Date(d.getTime() + DateRange.DAY);
    }
}

var now = new Date();
var tomorrow = new Date(now.getTime() + DateRange.DAY);
var nextweek = new Date(now.getTime() + 7*DateRange.DAY);
var week = new DateRange(now, nextweek);

week.includes(tomorrow)    // => true
week.foreach(function(d) { // Print each day in the week
    console.log(d.toLocaleDateString());
});
```

Augmenting Classes

JavaScript's prototype-based inheritance mechanism is dynamic: an object inherits properties from its prototype, even if the properties of the prototype change after the object is created. This means that we can augment JavaScript classes simply by adding new methods to their prototype objects. Here is code that adds a method to our Range class:

```
// Return a new range with negated endpoints
Range.prototype.negate = function() {
    return new Range(-this.to, -this.from);
};
```

The prototype object of built-in JavaScript classes is also "open" like this, which means that we can add methods to numbers, strings, arrays, functions, and so on. Here are some examples:

```
// Invoke the function f this many times, passing the
// iteration number. E.g., to print "hello" 3 times:
//    var n = 3;
//    n.times(function(n) { console.log(n + " hello"); });
Number.prototype.times = function(f, context) {
    var n = Number(this);
```

```
        for(var i = 0; i < n; i++) f.call(context, i);
    };

    // Define the ES5 String.trim() method if it does not
    // exist. This method trims space from the start and end.
    String.prototype.trim =
        String.prototype.trim || function() {
            if (!this) return this;
            return this.replace(/^\s+|\s+$/g, "");
        };

    // Return a function's name or "". If it has a name
    // property, use it. Otherwise, convert the function to
    // a string and extract the name from that.
    Function.prototype.getName = function() {
        return this.name ||
            this.toString().match(/function\s*([^(]*)\(/)[1];
    };
```

It is possible to add methods to Object.prototype, making them available on all objects. This is not recommended, however, because prior to ECMAScript 5, there is no way to make these add-on methods nonenumerable, and if you add properties to Object.prototype, those properties will be reported by all for/in loops.

CHAPTER 9

Regular Expressions

A *regular expression* is an object that describes a pattern of characters. The JavaScript RegExp class represents regular expressions, and both String and RegExp define methods that use regular expressions to perform powerful pattern-matching and search-and-replace functions on text. This chapter begins by defining the syntax that regular expressions use to describe textual patterns. It then moves on to describe the String and RegExp methods that use regular expressions.

Describing Patterns with Regular Expressions

In JavaScript, regular expressions are represented by RegExp objects. RegExp objects may be created with the `RegExp()` constructor, of course, but they are more often created using a special literal syntax. Just as string literals are specified as characters within quotation marks, regular expression literals are specified as characters within a pair of slash (/) characters. Thus, your JavaScript code may contain lines like this:

```
var pattern = /s$/;
```

This line creates a new RegExp object and assigns it to the variable **pattern**. This particular RegExp object matches any string that ends with the letter "s." This regular expression could have equivalently been defined with the `RegExp()` constructor like this:

```
var pattern = new RegExp("s$");
```

Regular-expression pattern specifications consist of a series of characters. Most characters, including all alphanumeric characters, simply describe characters to be matched literally. Thus, the regular expression /java/ matches any string that contains the substring "java." Other characters in regular expressions are not matched literally but have special significance. For example, the regular expression /s$/ contains two characters. The first, "s," matches itself literally. The second, "$," is a special metacharacter that matches the end of a string. Thus, this regular expression matches any string that contains the letter "s" as its last character.

The following sections describe the various characters and metacharacters used in JavaScript regular expressions.

Literal Characters

All alphabetic characters and digits match themselves literally in regular expressions. Certain nonalphabetic characters can be matched literally with escape sequences. Table 9-1 lists these characters.

Table 9-1. Regular-expression literal characters

Character	Matches
Alphanumeric character	Itself
\0	The NUL character (\u0000)
\t	Tab (\u0009)
\n	Newline (\u000A)
\v	Vertical tab (\u000B)
\f	Form feed (\u000C)
\r	Carriage return (\u000D)

Character	Matches
\x *nn*	The Latin character specified by the hexadecimal number *nn*; for example, \x0A is the same as \n
\u *xxxx*	The Unicode character specified by the hexadecimal number *xxxx*; for example, \u0009 is the same as \t
\c *X*	The control character ^ *X*; for example, \cJ is equivalent to the newline character \n

A number of punctuation characters have special meanings in regular expressions. They are:

```
^ $ . * + ? = ! : | \ / ( ) [ ] { }
```

The meanings of these characters are discussed in the sections that follow. Some of these characters have special meaning only within certain contexts of a regular expression and are treated literally in other contexts. As a general rule, however, if you want to include any of these punctuation characters literally in a regular expression, you must precede them with a \. Other punctuation characters, such as quotation marks and @, do not have special meaning and simply match themselves literally in a regular expression.

Character Classes

Individual literal characters can be combined into *character classes* by placing them within square brackets. A character class matches any one character that is contained within it. Thus, the regular expression /[abc]/ matches any one of the letters a, b, or c. Negated character classes can also be defined; these match any character except those contained within the brackets. A negated character class is specified by placing a caret (^) as the first character inside the left bracket. The regexp /[^abc]/ matches any one character other than a, b, or c. Character classes can use a hyphen to indicate a range of characters. To match any one lowercase character from the Latin alphabet, use /[a-z]/, and to match any letter or digit from the Latin alphabet, use /[a-zA-Z0-9]/. Character classes work with Unicode characters as well. To match a Cyrillic character, for example, use /[\u0400-\u04FF]/.

The regular-expression syntax includes shortcuts for a few commonly used character classes. Table 9-2 lists these characters and summarizes character-class syntax.

Table 9-2. Regular expression character classes

Character	Matches
[...]	Any one character between the brackets.
[^...]	Any one character not between the brackets.
.	Any character except newline or another Unicode line terminator.
\w	Any ASCII word character. Equivalent to [a-zA-Z0-9_].
\W	Any character that is not an ASCII word character. Equivalent to [^a-zA-Z0-9_].
\s	Any Unicode whitespace character.
\S	Any character that is not Unicode whitespace. Note that \w and \S are not the same thing.
\d	Any ASCII digit. Equivalent to [0-9].
\D	Any character other than an ASCII digit. Equivalent to [^0-9].
[\b]	A literal backspace (special case).

Note that the special character-class escapes can be used within square brackets. \s matches any whitespace character, and \d matches any digit, so /[\s\d]/ matches any one whitespace character or digit.

Repetition

A character or character class may be followed by additional characters that specify how many times those characters should be matched. Table 9-3 summarizes the repetition syntax.

Table 9-3. Regular expression repetition characters

Character	Meaning
{n ,m}	Match the previous item at least *n* times but no more than *m* times.
{n ,}	Match the previous item *n* or more times.
{n}	Match exactly *n* occurrences of the previous item.
?	Match zero or one occurrences of the previous item. That is, the previous item is optional. Equivalent to {0,1}.
+	Match one or more occurrences of the previous item. Equivalent to {1, }.
*	Match zero or more occurrences of the previous item. Equivalent to {0, }.

The following lines show some examples:

```
/\d{2,4}/    // Between two and four digits
/\w{3}\d?/   // Three word characters + optional digit
/\s+java\s+/ // "java" with spaces before and after
/[^(]*/      // zero or more chars that are not '('
```

Be careful when using the * and ? repetition characters. Since these characters may match zero instances of whatever precedes them, they are allowed to match nothing. For example, the regular expression /a*/ actually matches the string "bbbb" because the string contains zero occurrences of the letter a!

Nongreedy repetition

The repetition characters listed in Table 9-3 match as many times as possible while still allowing any following parts of the regular expression to match. We say that this repetition is "greedy." It is also possible to specify that repetition should be done in a nongreedy way. Simply follow the repetition character or characters with a question mark: ??, +?, *?, or even {1,5}?. For example, the regular expression /a+/ matches one or more occurrences of the letter a. When applied to the string "aaa," it matches all three letters. But /a+?/ matches one or more occurrences of the letter a, matching as few characters as necessary. When applied to the same string, this pattern matches only the first letter a.

Alternation, Grouping, and References

The regular-expression grammar includes special characters for specifying alternatives, grouping subexpressions, and referring to previous subexpressions. The | character separates alternatives. For example, /ab|cd|ef/ matches the string "ab" or the string "cd" or the string "ef." And /\d{3}|[a-z]{4}/ matches either three digits or four lowercase letters.

Note that alternatives are considered left to right until a match is found. If the left alternative matches, the right alternative is ignored, even if it would have produced a "better" match. Thus, when the pattern /a|ab/ is applied to the string "ab," it matches only the first letter.

Parentheses have several purposes in regular expressions. One is to group separate items into a subexpression so the items can be treated as a single unit by |, *, +, ?, and so on. For example, /java(script)?/ matches "java" followed by the optional "script." And /(ab|cd)+|ef/ matches either the string "ef" or one or more repetitions of either of the strings "ab" or "cd."

Another purpose of parentheses is to define subpatterns within the complete pattern. When a regular expression is successfully matched against a target string, you can extract the portions of the target string that matched any particular parenthesized subpattern. (You'll see how these matching substrings are obtained later.) For example, suppose you're looking for one or more lowercase letters followed by one or more digits. You might use the pattern /[a-z]+\d+/. But suppose you only care about the digits at the end of each match. If you put that part of the pattern in parentheses (/[a-z]+(\d+)/), you can extract the digits from any matches you find, as explained later.

A related use of parenthesized subexpressions is to allow you to refer back to a subexpression later in the same regular expression. This is done by following a \ character by a digit or digits. The digits refer to the position of the parenthesized subexpression within the regular expression. For example, \3 refers back to the third subexpression.

A reference to a previous subexpression of a regular expression does *not* refer to the pattern for that subexpression but rather to the text that matched the pattern. Thus, references can be used to enforce a constraint that separate portions of a string contain exactly the same characters. For example, the following regular expression matches zero or more characters within single or double quotes. However, it does not require the opening and closing quotes to match (i.e., both single quotes or both double quotes):

```
/['"][^'"]*['"]/
```

To require the quotes to match, use a reference:

```
/(['"])[^'"]*\1/
```

The **\1** matches whatever the first parenthesized subexpression matched. In this example, it enforces the constraint that the closing quote match the opening quote.

It is also possible to group items in a regular expression without creating a numbered reference to those items. Instead of simply grouping the items within (and), begin the group with (?: and end it with).

Table 9-4. Regular expression alternation, grouping, and reference characters

Character	Meaning
|	Alternation. Match either the subexpression to the left or the subexpression to the right.
(...)	Grouping. Group items into a single unit that can be used with *, +, ?, |, and so on. Also remember the characters that match this group for use with later references.
(?:...)	Grouping only. Group items into a single unit, but do not remember the characters that match this group.
\n	Match the same characters that were matched when group number *n* was first matched. Groups are subexpressions within (possibly nested) parentheses. Group numbers are assigned by counting left parentheses from left to right. Groups formed with (?: are not numbered.

Specifying Match Position

As described earlier, many elements of a regular expression match a single character in a string. For example, \s matches a single character of whitespace. Other regular expression elements match the positions between characters, instead of actual characters. \b, for example, matches a word boundary—the boundary between a \w (ASCII word character) and a \W (nonword character), or the boundary between an ASCII word character and the beginning or end of a string. Elements such as \b do not specify any characters to be used in a matched string; what they do specify, however, are legal positions at which a match can occur. Sometimes these elements are called *anchors* because they anchor the pattern to a specific position in the search string. The most commonly used anchor elements are ^, which ties the pattern to the beginning of the string, and $, which anchors the pattern to the end of the string.

For example, to match the word "JavaScript" on a line by itself, you can use the regular expression /^JavaScript$/. If you want to search for "Java" as a word by itself (not as a prefix, as it is in "JavaScript"), you can try the pattern /\sJava\s/, which requires a space before and after the word. But there are two problems with this solution. First, it does not match "Java" at the beginning or the end of a string, but only if it appears with space on either side. Second, when this pattern does find a match, the matched string it returns has leading and trailing spaces, which is not quite what's needed. So instead of matching actual space characters with \s, match (or anchor to) word boundaries with \b. The resulting expression is /\bJava\b/. The element \B anchors the match to a location that is not a word boundary. Thus, the pattern /\B[Ss]cript/ matches "JavaScript" and "postscript," but not "script" or "Scripting."

Table 9-5 summarizes regular-expression anchors.

Table 9-5. Regular-expression anchor characters

Character	Meaning
^	Match the beginning of the string and, in multiline searches, the beginning of a line.
$	Match the end of the string and, in multiline searches, the end of a line.
\b	Match a word boundary. That is, match the position between a \w character and a \W character or between a \w character and the beginning or end of a string. (Note, however, that [\b] matches backspace.)
\B	Match a position that is not a word boundary.
(?=p)	A positive lookahead assertion. Require that the following characters match the pattern *p*, but do not include those characters in the match.
(?!p)	A negative lookahead assertion. Require that the following characters do not match the pattern *p*.

Flags

There is one final element of regular-expression grammar. Regular-expression flags specify high-level pattern-matching rules. Unlike the rest of regular-expression syntax, flags are specified to the right of the second slash. JavaScript supports three flags. The i flag specifies that pattern matching should be case-insensitive. The g flag specifies that pattern matching should be global—that is, all matches within the searched string should be found. The m flag performs pattern matching in multiline mode. In this mode, if the string to be searched contains newlines, the ^ and $ anchors match the beginning and end of a line in addition to matching the beginning and end of a string. These flags may be specified in any combination. For example, the pattern /java$/im matches "java" as well as "Java\nis fun."

Table 9-6 summarizes these regular-expression flags. Note that you'll see more about the g flag in the next section.

Table 9-6. Regular-expression flags

Character	Meaning
i	Perform case-insensitive matching.
g	Perform a global match—that is, find all matches rather than stopping after the first match.
m	Multiline mode. ^ matches beginning of line or beginning of string, and $ matches end of line or end of string.

Matching Patterns with Regular Expressions

This section discusses methods of the String and RegExp objects that use regular expressions to perform pattern matching and search-and-replace operations.

String Methods for Pattern-Matching

Strings support four methods that use regular expressions. The simplest is search(). This method takes a regular-expression argument and returns either the character position of the start of the first matching substring or –1 if there is no match. For example, the following call returns 4:

```
"JavaScript".search(/script/i);
```

search() does not support global searches; it ignores the g flag of its regular-expression argument.

The replace() method performs a search-and-replace operation. It takes a regular expression as its first argument and a replacement string as its second argument. It searches the string on which it is called for matches with the specified pattern. If the regular expression has the g flag set, the replace() method replaces all matches in the string with the replacement string; otherwise, it replaces only the first match it finds. If the first argument to replace() is a string rather than a regular expression, the method searches for that string literally rather than converting it to a regular expression with the `RegExp()` constructor, as `search()` does. As an example, you can use `replace()` as follows to provide uniform capitalization of the word "JavaScript" throughout a string of text:

```
text.replace(/javascript/gi, "JavaScript");
```

`replace()` is more powerful than this, however. Recall that parenthesized subexpressions of a regular expression are numbered from left to right and that the regular expression remembers the text that each subexpression matches. If a `$` followed by a digit appears in the replacement string, `replace()` replaces those two characters with the text that matches the specified subexpression. You can use this feature, for example, to replace straight quotes in a string with curly quotes, simulated with ASCII characters:

```
// A quote is a quotation mark, followed by any number
// of nonquotation-mark characters (which we remember),
// followed by another quotation mark.
var quote = /"([^"]*)"/g;
// Replace the straight quotation marks with curly quotes,
// leaving the quoted text (stored in $1) unchanged.
text.replace(quote, '"$1"');
```

The second argument to `replace()` can also be a function that dynamically computes the replacement string. If you pass a function, it will be invoked once for each match. Its first argument will be the text of the matched string, and its remaining arguments will be the text that matched each parenthesized subexpression within the pattern. The return value of the function is used as the replacement string.

The `match()` method is the most general of the String regular-expression methods. It takes a regular expression as its only argument and returns an array that contains the results of the match. If the regular expression has the **g** flag set, the method returns an array of all matches that appear in the string. For example:

```
"1 plus 2 equals 3".match(/\d+/g)  // => ["1","2","3"]
```

If the regular expression does not have the g flag set, match() does not do a global search; it simply searches for the first match. However, match() returns an array even when it does not perform a global search. In this case, the first element of the array is the matching string, and any remaining elements are the substrings that matched the parenthesized subexpressions of the regular expression. To draw a parallel with the replace() method, a[n] holds the contents of $n.

For example, consider parsing a URL with the following code:

```
var url = /(\w+):\/\/([\w.]+)\/(\S*)/;
var text = "Visit http://www.example.com/~david";
var result = text.match(url);
if (result != null) {
    var fullurl = result[0];  // the complete match
    var protocol = result[1]; // => "http"
    var host = result[2];     // => "www.example.com"
    var path = result[3];     // => "~david"
}
```

The last of the regular-expression methods of the String object is split(). This method breaks the string on which it is called into an array of substrings, using the argument as a separator. For example:

```
"123,456,789".split(",");  // => ["123","456","789"]
```

The split() method can also take a regular expression as its argument. This ability makes the method more powerful. For example, you can specify a separator character that allows an arbitrary amount of whitespace on either side:

```
"1 , 2,3".split(/\s*,\s*/); // => ["1","2","3"]
```

RegExp Properties and Methods

Each RegExp object has five properties. The source property contains the text of the regular expression. The global property specifies whether the regular expression has the g flag. The ignoreCase property specifies whether the regular expression has the i flag. The multiline property specifies whether the regular expression has the m flag. The final property is `lastIndex`, a read/write integer. For patterns with the g flag, this property stores the position in the string at which the next search is to begin. It is used by the `exec()` and `test()` methods, described below.

RegExp objects define two methods that perform pattern-matching operations; they behave similarly to the String methods described earlier. The main RegExp pattern-matching method is `exec()`. It is similar to the String `match()` method described in "Matching Patterns with Regular Expressions" on page 158, except that it is a RegExp method that takes a string, rather than a String method that takes a RegExp. The `exec()` method executes a regular expression on the specified string. That is, it searches the string for a match. If it finds none, it returns `null`. If it does find one, however, it returns an array just like the array returned by the `match()` method for nonglobal searches. Element 0 of the array contains the string that matched the regular expression, and any subsequent array elements contain the substrings that matched any parenthesized subexpressions. Furthermore, the `index` property contains the character position at which the match occurred, and the `input` property refers to the string that was searched.

Unlike the `match()` method, `exec()` returns the same kind of array whether or not the regular expression has the global g flag. Recall that `match()` returns an array of matches when passed a global regular expression. `exec()`, by contrast, always returns a single match and provides complete information about that match. When `exec()` is called on a regular expression that has the g flag, it sets the `lastIndex` property of the regular-expression object to the character position immediately following the matched substring. When `exec()` is invoked a second time for the same regular expression, it begins its search at the character position indicated by the `lastIndex` property. If `exec()` does not find a match, it resets `lastIndex` to 0. (You can also set `lastIndex` at any time.) This special behavior allows you to call `exec()` repeatedly in order to loop through all the regular expression matches in a string.

For example:

```
var pattern = /Java/g;
var text = "JavaScript is more fun than Java!";
var result;
while((result = pattern.exec(text)) != null) {
    alert("Matched '" + result[0] + "'" +
            " at position " + result.index +
            "; next search at " + pattern.lastIndex);
}
```

The other RegExp method is **test()**. **test()** is a much simpler method than **exec()**. It takes a string and returns **true** if the string contains a match for the regular expression:

```
var pattern = /java/i;
pattern.test("JavaScript");  // Returns true
```

Calling **test()** is equivalent to calling **exec()** and returning **true** if the return value of **exec()** is not **null**. Because of this equivalence, the **test()** method behaves the same way as the **exec()** method when invoked for a global regular expression: it begins searching the specified string at the position specified by **lastIndex**, and if it finds a match, it sets **lastIndex** to the position of the character immediately following the match. Thus, you can loop through a string using the **test()** method just as you can with the **exec()** method.

CHAPTER 10

Client-Side JavaScript

The first part of this book described the core JavaScript language. We now move on to JavaScript as used within web browsers, commonly called client-side JavaScript. Most of the examples we've seen so far, while legal JavaScript code, have no particular context; they are JavaScript fragments that run in no specified environment. This chapter introduces that context, and the chapters that follow fill in the details.

Embedding JavaScript in HTML

JavaScript code can appear inline within an HTML file between `<script>` and `</script>` tags:

```
<script>
// Your JavaScript code goes here
</script>
```

Example 10-1 is an HTML file that includes a simple JavaScript program. The comments explain what the program does, but the main point of this example is to demonstrate how JavaScript code is embedded within an HTML file along with, in this case, a CSS stylesheet.

Example 10-1. A simple JavaScript digital clock

```
<!DOCTYPE html> <!-- This is an HTML5 file -->
<html>          <!-- The root element -->
```

```
<head>              <!-- Title, scripts & styles go here -->
<title>Digital Clock</title>
<script>            // A script of js code
// Define a function to display the current time
function displayTime() {
    var now = new Date(); // Get current time
    // Find element with id="clock"
    var elt = document.getElementById("clock");
    // Display the time in the element
    elt.innerHTML = now.toLocaleTimeString();
    // And repeat in one second
    setTimeout(displayTime, 1000);
}
// Start the clock when the document loads.
window.onload = displayTime;
</script>
<style>             /* A CSS stylesheet for the clock */
#clock {           /* Styles apply to element with id="clock" */
  font: bold 24pt sans;     /* Use a big bold font */
  background: #ddf;         /* on a light gray background. */
  padding: 10px;           /* Surround it with some space */
  border: solid black 2px; /* and a solid black border */
  border-radius: 10px;     /* with rounded corners. */
}
</style>
</head>
<body>             <!-- Content goes here. -->
<h1>Digital Clock</h1>    <!-- A title -->
<span id="clock"></span> <!-- Time inserted here -->
</body>
</html>
```

The `<script>` tag can also be used with a `src` attribute that
specifies the URL of a file containing JavaScript code. It is used
like this:

```
<script src="../../scripts/util.js"></script>
```

A JavaScript file contains pure JavaScript, without `<script>`
tags or any other HTML. By convention, files of JavaScript
code have names that end with *.js*.

A `<script>` tag with the `src` attribute specified behaves exactly
as if the contents of the specified JavaScript file appeared directly between the `<script>` and `</script>` tags. Note that the
closing `</script>` tag is required in HTML documents even

when the `src` attribute is specified, and there is no content between the `<script>` and `</script>` tags.

JavaScript was the original scripting language for the Web and `<script>` elements are, by default, assumed to contain or to reference JavaScript code. `<script>` elements have a `type` attribute whose default value is "text/javascript." You can specify this type explicitly if you want, but it is never necessary.

Event-Driven Programming

Client-side JavaScript programs are generally asynchronous and event-driven. When a web page loads, the scripts in that web page generally initialize some variables and register some event handler functions. These functions are then invoked by the browser when the events for which they were registered occur. A web application that wants to enable keyboard shortcuts for common actions would register an event handler for key events, for example. Even noninteractive programs use events. Suppose you wanted to write a program that would analyze the structure of its document and automatically generate a table of contents for the document. No event handlers for user input events are necessary, but the program would still register an `onload` event handler so that it would know when the document had finished loading and was ready to have a table of contents generated.

Events and event handling are the subject of Chapter 12.

The Window Object

The Window object is the main entry point to all client-side JavaScript features and APIs. It represents a web browser window or frame, and you can refer to it with the identifier `window`. The Window object defines properties like `location`, which refers to a Location object that specifies the URL currently displayed in the window and allows a script to load a new URL into the window:

```
// Set location to navigate to a new web page
window.location = "http://www.oreilly.com/";
```

The Window object also defines methods like `alert()`, which displays a message in a dialog box, and `setTimeout()`, which registers a function to be invoked after a specified amount of time:

```
// Wait 2 seconds and then say hello
setTimeout(function() { alert("hello"); }, 2000);
```

Notice that the code above does not explicitly use the `window` property. In client-side JavaScript, the Window object is also the global object. This means that the Window object is at the top of the scope chain and that its properties and methods are effectively global variables and global functions. The Window object has a property named `window` that always refers to itself. You can use this property if you need to refer to the window object itself, but it is not usually necessary to use `window` if you just want to refer to access properties of the global window object.

As the global object, Window defines an assortment of properties and methods for client-side JavaScript programming. The most important of these is the `document` property, which is the subject of Chapter 11. The other properties and methods are covered in the subsections below.

Timers

`setTimeout()` and `setInterval()` allow you to register a function to be invoked once or repeatedly after a specified amount of time has elapsed. These are important global functions of client-side JavaScript, and are therefore defined as methods of Window, but they are general-purpose functions and don't really have anything to do with the window.

The `setTimeout()` method of the Window object schedules a function to run after a specified number of milliseconds elapses. `setTimeout()` returns a value that can be passed to `clearTimeout()` to cancel the execution of the scheduled function.

If you call setTimeout() with a time of 0 ms, the function you specify is not invoked right away. Instead, it is placed on a queue to be invoked "as soon as possible" after any currently pending event handlers finish running.

setInterval() is like setTimeout() except that the specified function is invoked repeatedly at intervals of the specified number of milliseconds:

```
// Call updateClock() every 60 seconds
setInterval(updateClock, 60000);
```

Like setTimeout(), setInterval() returns a value that can be passed to clearInterval() to cancel any future invocations of the scheduled function.

Browser Location and Navigation

The location property of the Window object refers to a Location object, which represents the current URL of the document displayed in the window, and which also defines methods for making the window load a new document.

The location property of a window is a reference to a Location object; it represents the current URL of the document being displayed in that window. The href property of the Location object is a string that contains the complete text of the URL. The toString() method of the Location object returns the value of the href property, so you can usually just write location rather than location.href.

Other properties of this object—protocol, host, hostname, port, pathname, search, and hash—specify the individual parts of the URL. They are known as "URL decomposition" properties, and they are also supported by Link objects (created by <a> and <area> elements in HTML documents).

The Location object also defines a reload(), which makes the browser reload the document.

The Location object can also be used to make the browser navigate to a new page: simply assign the new URL directly to the `location` property:

```
location = "http://www.oreilly.com";
```

You can also assign relative URLs to `location`. They are resolved against the current URL:

```
location = "page2.html"; // Next page
```

A bare fragment identifier is a special kind of relative URL that does not cause the browser to load a new document but simply scroll to display a new section of the document. The identifier `#top` is a special case: if no document element has the ID "top," it makes the browser jump to the start of the document:

```
location = "#top";
```

The URL decomposition properties of the Location object are writable, and setting them changes the location URL and also causes the browser to load a new document (or, in the case of the `hash` property, to navigate within the current document):

```
location.search = "?page=" + (pagenum+1);
```

Browsing History

The `history` property of the Window object refers to the History object for the window. The History object models the browsing history of a window as a list of documents and document states.

The History object has `back()` and `forward()` methods that behave like the browser's Back and Forward buttons do: they make the browser go backward or forward one step in its browsing history. A third method, `go()`, takes an integer argument and can skip any number of pages forward (for positive arguments) or backward (for negative arguments) in the history list:

```
history.go(-2); // Like clicking Back twice
```

If a window contains child windows (such as `<iframe>` elements—see "Relationships Between Frames" on page 173), the browsing histories of the child windows are chronologically interleaved with the history of the main window. This means that calling `history.back()` (for example) on the main window may cause one of the child windows to navigate back to a previously displayed document but leave the main window in its current state.

Modern web applications can dynamically alter their own content without loading a new document. Applications that do this may want to allow the user to use the Back and Forward buttons to navigate between these dynamically created application states. One way to do this is to store application state by setting `location.hash` to a string that captures the application's current state. Even though this does not load a new document, it creates a new history entry, and if the user later uses the Back button to go back to that history entry, the browser will fire a "hashchange" event. An application that wants to track the Forward and Back buttons can register a handler by setting `window.onhashchange`.

Another more complicated way of managing the browsing history for a web application involves the `history.pushState()` method and its corresponding `window.onpopstate` event handler. Coverage of that API is beyond the scope of this book, however.

Browser and Screen Information

Scripts sometimes need to obtain information about the web browser in which they are running or the desktop on which the browser appears. This section describes the `navigator` and `screen` properties of the Window object. Those properties refer to Navigator and Screen objects, respectively, and these objects provide information that allows a script to customize its behavior based on its environment.

The `navigator` property of a Window object refers to a Navigator object that contains browser vendor and version number information. The Navigator object is named after the early Navigator browser from Netscape, but it is also supported by all other browsers.

The Navigator object has four properties that provide information about the browser that is running:

appName
> The full name of the web browser. In IE, this is "Microsoft Internet Explorer." In Firefox, this property is "Netscape." For compatibility, other browsers often report the name "Netscape" as well.

appVersion
> This property typically begins with a number and follows that with a detailed string that contains browser vendor and version information. The number at the start of this string is often 4.0 or 5.0 to indicate generic compatibility with fourth- and fifth-generation browsers. There is no standard format for the appVersion string, so parsing it in a browser-independent way isn't possible.

userAgent
> The string that the browser sends in its USER-AGENT HTTP header. This property typically contains all the information in appVersion and may contain additional details as well. Like appVersion, there is no standard format.

platform
> A string that identifies the operating system (and possibly the hardware) on which the browser is running.

In addition to its browser vendor and version information properties, the Navigator object has some miscellaneous properties and methods. The standardized and widely implemented nonstandard properties include:

onLine
> The navigator.onLine property (if it exists) specifies whether the browser is currently connected to the network.

---

geolocation

> A Geolocation object that defines an API for determining the user's geographical location. The details of this API are beyond the scope of this pocket reference.

The **screen** property of a Window object refers to a Screen object that provides information about the size of the user's display. The **width** and **height** properties specify the size of the display in pixels. The **availWidth** and **availHeight** properties specify the display size that is actually available; they exclude the space required by features such as a desktop taskbar. You might use the Screen object to determine whether your web app is running in a small form factor device such as a tablet or mobile phone.

Dialog Boxes

The Window object provides three methods for displaying simple dialog boxes to the user. **alert()** displays a message to the user and waits for the user to dismiss the dialog. **con firm()** displays a message, waits for the user to click an OK or Cancel button and returns a boolean value. And **prompt()** displays a message, waits for the user to enter a string, and returns that string. The following code uses all three methods:

```
do {
  // Ask for a string
  var n = prompt("What is your name?");
  // Ask for a confirmation
  var ok = confirm("Is " + n + " okay?");
} while(!ok)
alert("Hello, " + n); // Display a greeting
```

Although the **alert()**, **confirm()**, and **prompt()** methods are very easy to use, good design dictates that you use them sparingly, if at all. Dialog boxes like these are not a common feature on the Web, and most users will find the dialog boxes produced by these methods disruptive to their browsing experience.

Document Elements as Window Properties

If you name an element in your HTML document using the `id` attribute, and if the Window object does not already have a property by that name, the Window object is given a nonenumerable property whose name is the value of the `id` attribute and whose value is the HTMLElement object that represents that document element.

As we've already noted, the Window object serves as the global object in client-side JavaScript, so this means that the `id` attributes you use in your HTML documents become global variables (if there are not already variables by those names) accessible to your scripts. If your document includes the element `<button id="okay"/>`, you can refer to that element using the global variable `okay`.

The implicit use of element IDs as global variables is a historical quirk of web browser evolution. It is required for backward compatibility with existing web pages, but its use is not recommended. Instead, explicitly look up elements using the techniques shown in Chapter 11.

Multiple Windows and Frames

A single web browser window on your desktop may contain several tabs. Each tab is an independent *browsing context*. Each has its own Window object, and each is isolated from all the others. The scripts running in one tab usually have no way of even knowing that the other tabs exist, much less of interacting with their Window objects or manipulating their document content. If you use a web browser that does not support tabs, or if you have tabs turned off, you may have many web browser windows open on your desktop at one time. As with tabs, each desktop window has its own Window object, and each is usually independent of and isolated from all of the others.

HTML documents may contain nested documents using an `<iframe>` element. An `<iframe>` creates a nested browsing context represented by a Window object of its own. The deprecated `<frameset>` and `<frame>` elements also create nested browsing contexts, and each `<frame>` is represented by a Window. Client-side JavaScript makes very little distinction between windows, tabs, iframes, and frames: they are all browsing contexts, and to JavaScript, they are all Window objects. Nested browsing contexts are not isolated from one another the way independent tabs usually are. A script running in one frame can always see its ancestor and descendant frames, though the same-origin policy described in "The Same-Origin Policy" on page 176 may prevent the script from inspecting the documents in those frames. Nested frames are the topic of "Relationships Between Frames" on page 173.

Since the Window is the global object of client-side JavaScript, each window or frame has a separate JavaScript execution context. Nevertheless, JavaScript code in one window can, subject to same-origin constraints, use the objects, properties, and methods defined in other windows. This is discussed in more detail in "JavaScript in Interacting Windows" on page 175.

Relationships Between Frames

You already know that the JavaScript code in any window or frame can refer to its own Window object as `window` (or as `self`). A frame can refer to the Window object of the window or frame that contains it using the `parent` property:

```
parent.history.back();
```

A Window object that represents a top-level window or tab has no container, and its `parent` property simply refers to the window itself:

```
parent == self; // For toplevel windows
```

If a frame is contained within another frame that is contained within a top-level window, that frame can refer to the top-level window as `parent.parent`. The `top` property is a general-case shortcut, however: no matter how deeply a frame is nested, its `top` property refers to the top-level containing window. If a Window object represents a top-level window, `top` simply refers to that window itself. For frames that are direct children of a top-level window, the `top` property is the same as the `parent` property.

The `parent` and `top` properties allow a script to refer to its frame's ancestors. There is more than one way to refer to the descendant frames of a window or frame. Frames are created with `<iframe>` elements. You can obtain an Element object that represents an `<iframe>` just as you would do for any other element. Suppose your document contains `<iframe id="f1">`. Then, the Element object that represents this iframe is:

```
var e = document.getElementById("f1");
```

`<iframe>` elements have a `contentWindow` property that refers to the Window object of the frame, so the Window object for this frame is:

```
var kid = document.getElementById("f1").contentWindow;
```

You can go in the reverse direction—from the Window that represents a frame to the `<iframe>` Element that contains the frame—with the `frameElement` property of the Window. Window objects that represent top-level windows rather than frames have a `null` `frameElement` property:

```
var elt = document.getElementById("f1");
var w = elt.contentWindow;
w.frameElement === elt  // Always true for frames
w.frameElement === null // For toplevel windows
```

It is not usually necessary to use the `getElementById()` method and the `contentWindow` property to obtain references to the child frames of a window, however. Every Window object has a `frames` property that refers to the child frames contained within the window or frame. The `frames` property refers to an array-like object that can be indexed numerically or by frame name. To refer to the first child frame of a window, you can use `frames[0]`. To refer to the third child frame of the second child, you can use `frames[1].frames[2]`. Code running in a frame might refer to a sibling frame as `parent.frames[1]`. Note that the elements of the `frames[]` array are Window objects, not `<iframe>` elements.

If you specify the `name` or `id` attribute of an `<iframe>` element, that frame can be indexed by name as well as by number. A frame named "f1" would be `frames["f1"]` or `frames.f1`, for example.

You can use the `name` or `id` attribute of an `<iframe>` element to give the frame a name that can be used in JavaScript code. If you use the `name` attribute, however, the name you specify also becomes the value of the `name` property of the Window that represents the frame. A name specified in this way can be used as the `target` attribute of a link.

JavaScript in Interacting Windows

Each window or frame is its own JavaScript execution context with a Window as its global object. But if code in one window or frame can refer to another window or frame (and if the same-origin policy does not prevent it), the scripts in one window or frame can interact with the scripts in the other.

Imagine a web page with two `<iframe>` elements named "A" and "B," and suppose that those frames contain documents from the same server and that those documents contain interacting scripts. The script in frame A might define a variable `i`:

```
var i = 3;
```

That variable is nothing more than a property of the global object—a property of the Window object. Code in frame A can refer to the variable with the identifier `i`, or it can explicitly reference it through the window object:

```
window.i
```

Since the script in frame B can refer to the Window object for frame A, it can also refer to the properties of that window object:

```
parent.A.i = 4;
```

Recall that the `function` keyword that defines functions creates a variable just like the `var` keyword does. If a script in frame B declares a function `f`, that function is a global variable in frame B, and code in frame B can invoke `f` as `f()`. Code in frame A, however, must refer to `f` as a property of the Window object of frame B:

```
parent.B.f();
```

If the code in frame A needs to use this function frequently, it might assign the function to a variable of frame A so that it can more conveniently refer to the function:

```
var f = parent.B.f;
```

Now code in frame A can invoke the function as `f()`, just as code in frame B does.

When you share functions between frames or windows like this, it is important to keep the rules of lexical scoping in mind. A function is executed in the scope in which it was defined, not in the scope from which it is invoked. Thus, if the function `f` above refers to global variables, these variables are looked up as properties of frame B, even when the function is invoked from frame A.

The Same-Origin Policy

The *same-origin policy* is a sweeping security restriction on what web content JavaScript code can interact with. It typically comes into play when a web page includes `<iframe>` elements. In this case, the same-origin policy governs the interactions of JavaScript code in one window or frame with the content of other windows and frames. Specifically, a script can read only the properties of windows and documents that have the same origin as the document that contains the script.

The *origin* of a document is defined as the protocol, host, and port of the URL from which the document was loaded. Documents loaded from different web servers have different origins. Documents loaded through different ports of the same host have different origins. And a document loaded with the `http:` protocol has a different origin than one loaded with the `https:` protocol, even if they come from the same web server.

It is important to understand that the origin of the script itself is not relevant to the same-origin policy: what matters is the origin of the document in which the script is embedded. Suppose, for example, that a script hosted by host A is included (using the `src` property of a `<script>` element) in a web page served by host B. The origin of that script is host B and the script has full access to the content of the document that contains it. If the script creates an iframe and loads a second document from host B into it, the script also has full access to the content of that second document. But if the script opens another iframe and loads a document from host C (or even one from host A) into it, the same-origin policy comes into effect and prevents the script from accessing this document.

The same-origin policy does not actually apply to all properties of all objects in a window from a different origin. But it does apply to many of them, and, in particular, it applies to practically all the properties of the Document object. You should consider any window or frame that contains a document from another server to be off-limits to your scripts.

The same-origin policy also applies to scripted HTTP requests made with the XMLHttpRequest object (see Chapter 13). This object allows client-side JavaScript code to make arbitrary HTTP requests to the web server from which the containing document was loaded, but it does not allow scripts to communicate with other web servers.

CHAPTER 11

Scripting Documents

Client-side JavaScript exists to turn static HTML documents into interactive web applications. The Document object represents the content of a web browser window, and it is the subject of this chapter. The Document object does not stand alone, however. It is the central object in a larger API, known as the *Document Object Model*, or DOM, for representing and manipulating document content.

Overview of the DOM

The Document Object Model, or DOM, is the fundamental API for representing and manipulating the content of HTML documents. The API is not particularly complicated, but there are a number of architectural details you need to understand. First, you should understand that the nested elements of an HTML or XML document are represented in the DOM as a tree of objects. The tree representation of an HTML document contains nodes representing HTML tags or elements, such as `<body>` and `<p>`, and nodes representing strings of text. An HTML document may also contain nodes representing HTML comments. Consider the following simple HTML document:

```
<html>
  <head>
    <title>Sample Document</title>
```

```
    </head>
    <body>
      <h1>An HTML Document</h1>
      <p>This is a <i>simple</i> document.
  </html>
```

The DOM representation of this document is the tree pictured in Figure 11-1.

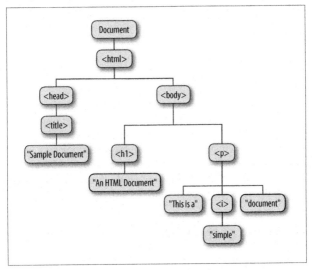

Figure 11-1. The tree representation of an HTML document

If you are not already familiar with tree structures in computer programming, it is helpful to know that they borrow terminology from family trees. The node directly above a node is the *parent* of that node. The nodes one level directly below another node are the *children* of that node. Nodes at the same level, and with the same parent, are *siblings*. The set of nodes any number of levels below another node are the *descendants* of that node. And the parent, grandparent, and all other nodes above a node are the *ancestors* of that node.

Each box in Figure 11-1 is a node of the document and is represented by a Node object. We'll talk about the properties and methods of Node in some of the sections that follow. Note that the figure contains three different types of nodes. At the root of the tree is the Document node that represents the entire document. The nodes that represent HTML elements are Element nodes, and the nodes that represent text are Text nodes. Document, Element, and Text are subclasses of Node. Document and Element are the two most important DOM classes, and much of this chapter is devoted to their properties and methods.

Node and its subtypes form the type hierarchy illustrated in Figure 11-2. Notice that there is a formal distinction between the generic Document and Element types, and the HTMLDocument and HTMLElement types. The Document type represents either an HTML or an XML document, and the Element class represents an element of such a document. The HTMLDocument and HTMLElement subclasses are specific to HTML documents and elements. In this book, we often use the generic class names Document and Element, even when referring to HTML documents.

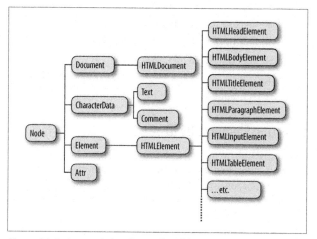

Figure 11-2. A partial class hierarchy of document nodes

It is also worth noting in Figure 11-2 that there are many sub-types of HTMLElement that represent specific types of HTML elements. Each defines JavaScript properties to mirror the HTML attributes of a specific element or group of elements. Some of these element-specific classes define additional properties or methods that go beyond simple mirroring of HTML syntax.

Selecting Document Elements

Most client-side JavaScript programs work by somehow manipulating one or more document elements. When these programs start, they can use the global variable `document` to refer to the Document object. In order to manipulate elements of the document, however, they must somehow obtain or *select* the Element objects that refer to those document elements. The DOM defines a number of ways to select elements; you can query a document for an element or elements:

- with a specified `id` attribute;
- with a specified `name` attribute;
- with the specified tag name;
- with the specified CSS class or classes; or
- matching the specified CSS selector

The subsections that follow explain each of these element selection techniques.

Selecting Elements by ID

Any HTML element can have an `id` attribute. The value of this attribute must be unique within the document—no two elements in the same document can have the same ID. You can select an element based on this unique ID with the `getElementById()` method of the Document object:

```
var sect1 = document.getElementById("section1");
```

This is the simplest and most commonly used way to select elements. If your script is going to manipulate a certain specific set of document elements, give those elements **id** attributes, and look up the Element objects using that ID. If you need to look up more than one element by ID, you might find the **getElements()** function of Example 11-1 useful.

Example 11-1. Looking up multiple elements by ID

```
/*
 * This function expects any number of string arguments.
 * It treats each argument as an element id and calls
 * document.getElementById() for each. It returns an
 * object that maps ids to matching Element objects.
 */
function getElements(/*ids...*/) {
    var elements = {};          // Start with empty map
    for(var i = 0; i < arguments.length; i++) {
        var id = arguments[i]; // Argument is an elt id
        var elt = document.getElementById(id);
        if (elt == null)
            throw new Error("No element with id: " + id);
        elements[id] = elt;     // Map id to element
    }
    return elements;            // Return id to elt map
}
```

Selecting Elements by Name

The HTML **name** attribute was originally intended to assign names to form elements, and the value of this attribute is used when form data is submitted to a server. Like the **id** attribute, **name** assigns a name to an element. Unlike **id**, however, the value of a **name** attribute does not have to be unique: multiple elements may have the same name, and this is common in the case of radio buttons and checkboxes in forms. Also, unlike **id**, the **name** attribute is only valid on a handful of HTML elements, including forms, form elements, `<iframe>`, and `<img>` elements.

To select HTML elements based on the value of their **name** attributes, you can use the **getElementsByName()** method of the Document object:

```
var btns = document.getElementsByName("color");
```

`getElementsByName()` returns a NodeList object that behaves like a read-only array of Element objects.

Setting the name attribute of a `<form>`, `<img>`, or `<iframe>`, creates a property of the Document object whose name is the value of the attribute (assuming, of course, that the document does not already have a property with that name). If there is only a single element with a given name, the value of the automatically created document property is the element itself. If there is more than one element, then the value of the property is a NodeList object that acts as an array of elements. The document properties created for named `<iframe>` elements are special: instead of referring to the Element object, they refer to the frame's Window object.

What this means is that some elements can be selected by name simply by using the name as a Document property:

```
// Get the object for <form name="shipping_address">
var form = document.shipping_address;
```

Selecting Elements by Type

You can select all elements of a specified type (or tag name) using the `getElementsByTagName()` method of the Document object. To obtain a read-only array-like object containing the Element objects for all `<span>` elements in a document, for example, you might write:

```
var spans = document.getElementsByTagName("span");
```

Like `getElementsByName()`, `getElementsByTagName()` returns a NodeList object. The elements of the returned NodeList are in document order, so you can select the first `<p>` element of a document like this:

```
var firstpara = document.getElementsByTagName("p")[0];
```

HTML tags are case-insensitive, and when `getElementsByTag Name()` is used on an HTML document, it performs a case-insensitive tag name comparison. The spans variable above, for

---

example, will include any `<span>` elements that were written as `<SPAN>`.

You can obtain a NodeList that represents all elements in a document by passing the wildcard argument "*" to `getElementsByTagName()`.

The Element class also defines a `getElementsByTagName()` method. It works in the same way as the Document version, but it only selects elements that are descendants of the element on which it is invoked. So to find all `<span>` elements inside the first `<p>` element of a document, you could write:

```
var firstp= document.getElementsByTagName("p")[0];
var firstpSpans = firstp.getElementsByTagName("span");
```

For historical reasons, the HTMLDocument class defines shortcut properties to access certain kinds of nodes. The `images`, `forms`, and `links` properties, for example, refer to objects that behave like read-only arrays of `<img>`, `<form>`, and `<a>` elements (but only `<a>` tags that have an `href` attribute). These properties refer to HTMLCollection objects, which are much like NodeList objects, but they can additionally be indexed by element ID or name. Earlier, we saw how you could refer to a named `<form>` element with an expression like this:

```
document.shipping_address
```

With the `document.forms` property, you can also refer more specifically to the named (or ID'ed) form like this:

```
document.forms.shipping_address;
```

HTMLDocument also defines two properties that refer to special single elements rather than element collections. `document.body` is the `<body>` element of an HTML document, and `document.head` is the `<head>` element. The `documentElement` property of the Document class refers to the root element of the document. In HTML documents, this is always an `<html>` element.

NodeLists and HTMLCollections

`getElementsByName()` and `getElementsByTagName()` return NodeList objects, and properties like `document.images` and `document.forms` are HTMLCollection objects.

These objects are read-only array-like objects. They have `length` properties and can be indexed (for reading but not writing) like true arrays. You can iterate the contents of a NodeList or HTMLCollection with a standard loop like this:

```
// Loop through all images and hide them
for(var i = 0; i < document.images.length; i++)
    document.images[i].style.display = "none";
```

One of the most important and surprising features of NodeList and HTMLCollection is that they are not static snapshots of a historical document state but are generally *live*, and the list of elements they contain can vary as the document changes. Suppose you call `getElementsByTagName('div')` on a document with no `<div>` elements. The return value is a NodeList with a length of 0. If you then insert a new `<div>` element into the document, that element automatically becomes a member of the NodeList, and the `length` property changes to 1.

Selecting Elements by CSS Class

The `class` attribute of an HTML is a space-separated list of zero or more identifiers. It describes a way to define sets of related document elements: any elements that have the same identifier in their `class` attribute are part of the same set. `class` is a reserved word in JavaScript, so client-side JavaScript uses the `className` property to hold the value of the HTML `class` attribute. The `class` attribute is usually used in conjunction with a CSS stylesheet to apply the same presentation styles to all members of a set. In addition, however, HTML5 defines a method, `getElementsByClassName()`, that allows us to select sets of document elements based on the identifiers in their `class` attribute.

Like getElementsByTagName(), getElementsByClassName() can be invoked on both HTML documents and HTML elements, and it returns a live NodeList containing all matching descendants of the document or element. getElementsByClassName() takes a single string argument, but the string may specify multiple space-separated identifiers. Only elements that include all of the specified identifiers in their class attribute are matched. The order of the identifiers does not matter. Here are some examples of getElementsByClassName():

```
// Find all elements with class "warning"
var w = document.getElementsByClassName("warning");
// Find descendants of the element "log" that have
// classes "error" and "fatal"
var log = document.getElementById("log");
var fatal = log.getElementsByClassName("fatal error");
```

Selecting Elements with CSS Selectors

CSS stylesheets have a very powerful syntax, known as *selectors*, for describing elements or sets of elements within a document. Full details of CSS selector syntax are beyond the scope of this book, but some examples will demonstrate the basics. Elements can be described by ID, tag name, or class:

```
#nav        // An element with id="nav"
div         // Any <div> element
.warning    // Any element with class "warning"
```

More generally, elements can be selected based on attribute values:

```
p[lang="fr"]  // A paragraph in French: <p lang="fr">
*[name="x"]   // Any element with name="x" attribute
```

These basic selectors can be combined:

```
span.fatal.error // <span> with classes "fatal" & "error"
span[lang="fr"].warning // Any warning in French
```

Selectors can also specify document structure:

```
#log span // Any <span> descendant of the log
#log>span // Any <span> child of the log
body>h1:first-child // The first <h1> child of <body>
```

Selectors can be combined to select multiple elements or multiple sets of elements:

```
div, #log // All <div> elements plus the log
```

As you can see, CSS selectors allow elements to be selected in all of the ways described above: by ID, by name, by tag name, and by class name. You can select elements that match a CSS selector with the Document method `querySelectorAll()`. It takes a single string argument containing a CSS selector and returns a NodeList that represents all elements in the document that match the selector. Unlike previously described element selection methods, the NodeList returned by `querySelectorAll()` is not live: it holds the elements that match the selector at the time the method was invoked, but it does not update as the document changes. If no elements match, `querySelectorAll()` returns an empty NodeList. If the selector string is invalid, `querySelectorAll()` throws an exception.

In addition to `querySelectorAll()`, the document object also defines `querySelector()`, which is like `querySelectorAll()`, but returns only the first (in document order) matching element or `null` if there is no matching element.

These two methods are also defined on Elements. When invoked on an element, the specified selector is matched against the entire document, and then the result set is filtered so that it only includes descendants of the specified element.

Document Structure and Traversal

Once you have selected an Element from a Document, you sometimes need to find structurally related portions (parent, siblings, children) of the document. The Document object, its Element objects, and the Text objects that represent runs of text in the document are all Node objects. Node defines the following important properties:

parentNode

> The Node that is the parent of this one, or `null` for nodes like the Document object that have no parent.

childNodes

> A read-only array-like object (a NodeList) that is a live representation of a Node's child nodes.

firstChild, lastChild

> The first and last child nodes of a node, or `null` if the node has no children.

nextSibling, previousSibling

> The next and previous sibling node of a node. Two nodes with the same parent are siblings. Their order reflects the order in which they appear in the document. These properties connect nodes in a doubly linked list.

nodeType

> The kind of node this is. Document nodes have the value 9. Element nodes have the value 1. Text nodes have the value 3. Comment nodes have the value 8.

nodeValue

> The textual content of a Text or Comment node.

nodeName

> The tag name of an Element, converted to uppercase.

Using these Node properties, the second child node of the first child of the Document can be referred to with expressions like these:

```
document.childNodes[0].childNodes[1]
document.firstChild.firstChild.nextSibling
```

Suppose the document in question is the following:

```
<html><head><title>Test</title></head><body>Hello!</body>
</html>
```

Then the second child of the first child is the `<body>` element. It has a **nodeType** of 1 and a **nodeName** of "BODY."

Note, however, that this API is extremely sensitive to variations in the document text. If the document is modified by inserting a single newline between the `<html>` and the `<head>` tag, for example, the Text node that represents that newline becomes the first child of the first child, and the second child is the `<head>` element instead of the `<body>` body.

When we are primarily interested in the Elements of a document instead of the text within them (and the whitespace between them), it is helpful to use an API that allows us to treat a document as a tree of Element objects, ignoring Text and Comment nodes that are also part of the document.

The first part of this API is the `children` property of Element objects. Like `childNodes`, this is a NodeList. Unlike `childNodes`, however, the `children` list contains only Element objects.

The second part of an element-based document traversal API is Element properties that are analogs to the child and sibling properties of the Node object:

`firstElementChild, lastElementChild`
> Like `firstChild` and `lastChild`, but for Element children only.

`nextElementSibling, previousElementSibling`
> Like `nextSibling` and `previousSibling`, but for Element siblings only.

`childElementCount`
> The number of Element children. Returns the same value as `children.length`.

Attributes

HTML elements consist of a tag name and a set of name/value pairs known as *attributes*. The `<a>` element that defines a hyperlink, for example, uses the value of its `href` attribute as the destination of the link. The attribute values of HTML elements are available as properties of the HTMLElement objects that represent those elements. The HTMLElement type defines properties for the universal HTTP attributes such as `id`, `title`, lang, and dir, and event handler properties like onclick. Element-specific subtypes define attributes specific to those elements. To query the URL of an image, for example, you can use the src property of the HTMLElement that represents the <img> element:

```
var img = document.getElementById("myimage");
var url = img.src; // The src attribute is the img URL
img.id = "myimg"    // Change the id attribute value
```

Similarly, you might set the form-submission attributes of a <form> element with code like this:

```
var f = document.forms[0]; // First <form> in doc
f.method = "POST"; // Post this form to url below
f.action = "http://www.example.com/submit.php";
```

HTML attributes are not case-sensitive, but JavaScript property names are. To convert an attribute name to the JavaScript property, write it in lowercase. If the attribute is more than one word long, however, put the first letter of each word after the first in uppercase: defaultChecked and tabIndex, for example.

Some HTML attribute names are reserved words in JavaScript. For these, the general rule is to prefix the property name with "html." The HTML for attribute (of the <label> element), for example, becomes the JavaScript htmlFor property. "class" is a reserved (but unused) word in JavaScript, and the very important HTML class attribute is an exception to the rule above: it becomes className in JavaScript code.

The properties that represent HTML attributes usually have a string value. When the attribute is a boolean or numeric value (the defaultChecked and maxLength attributes of an <input> element, for example), the properties values are booleans or numbers instead of strings. Event handler attributes always have Function objects (or null) as their values. The HTML5 specification defines a few attributes (such as the form attribute of <input> and related elements) that convert element IDs to actual Element objects.

As described above, HTMLElement and its subtypes define properties that correspond to the standard attributes of HTML elements. The Element type also defines `getAttribute()` and `setAttribute()` methods that you can use to query and set nonstandard HTML attributes:

```
var image = document.images[0];
var width = parseInt(image.getAttribute("WIDTH"));
image.setAttribute("class", "thumbnail");
```

The code above highlights two important differences between these methods and the property-based API described above. First, attribute values are all treated as strings. `getAttribute()` never returns a number, boolean, or object. Second, these methods use standard attribute names, even when those names are reserved words in JavaScript. For HTML elements, the attribute names are case-insensitive.

Element also defines two related methods, `hasAttribute()` and `removeAttribute()`, which check for the presence of a named attribute and remove an attribute entirely. These methods are particularly useful with boolean attributes: these are attributes (such as the `disabled` attribute of HTML form elements) whose presence or absence from an element matters but whose value is not relevant.

Element Content

Take a look again at Figure 11-1, and ask yourself what the "content" of the <p> element is. There are three ways we might answer this question:

- The content is the HTML string "This is a <i>simple</i> document."
- The content is the plain-text string "This is a simple document."
- The content is a Text node, an Element node that has a Text node child, and another Text node.

Each of these are valid answers, and each answer is useful in its own way. The sections that follow explain how to work with the HTML representation, the plain-text representation, and the tree representation of element content.

Element Content as HTML

Reading the `innerHTML` property of an Element returns the content of that element as a string of markup. Setting this property on an element invokes the web browser's parser and replaces the element's current content with a parsed representation of the new string.

Web browsers are very good at parsing HTML and setting `innerHTML` is usually fairly efficient, even though the value you specify must be parsed. Note, however, that repeatedly appending bits of text to the `innerHTML` property with the `+=` operator is usually not efficient because it requires both a serialization step and a parsing step.

The `insertAdjacentHTML()` method allows you to insert a string of arbitrary HTML markup "adjacent" to the specified element. The markup is passed as the second argument to this method, and the precise meaning of "adjacent" depends on the value of the first argument. This first argument should be a string with one of the values "beforebegin," "afterbegin," "beforeend," or "afterend." These values correspond to insertion points that are illustrated in Figure 11-3.

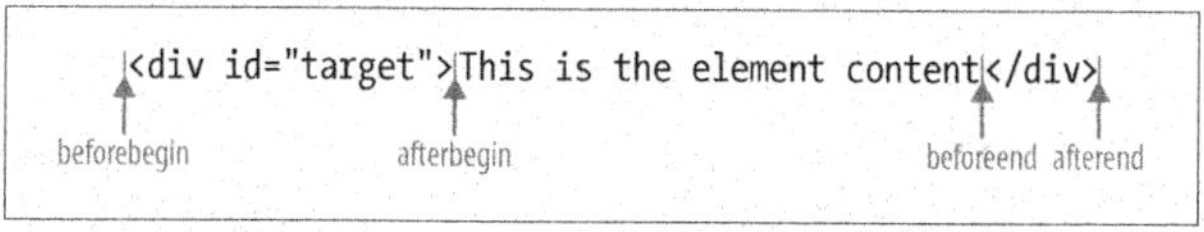

Figure 11-3. Insertion points for insertAdjacentHTML()

Element Content as Plain Text

Sometimes you want to query the content of an element as plain text, or to insert plain-text into a document (without having to escape the angle brackets and ampersands used in

HTML markup). The standard way to do this is with the text Content property of Node:

```
// Get first <p> in the document
var para = document.getElementsByTagName("p")[0];
// Get its text: "This is a simple document."
var text = para.textContent;
// Alter paragraph content
para.textContent = "Hello World!";
```

Element Content as Text Nodes

Another way to work with the content of an element is as a list of child nodes, each of which may have its own set of children. When thinking about element content, it is usually the Text nodes that are of interest.

Example 11-2 shows a textContent() function that recursively traverses the children of an element and concatenates the text of all the Text node descendants. In order to understand the code, recall that the nodeValue property (defined by the Node type) holds the content of a Text node.

Example 11-2. Finding all Text node descendants of an element

```
// Return the plain-text content of element e,
// recursing into child elements. This function works
// like the textContent property
function textContent(e) {
    var c, type, s = "";
    for(c=e.firstChild; c!=null; c=c.nextSibling) {
        type = c.nodeType;
        if (type === 3)          // Text node:
            s += c.nodeValue;    // add text content
        else if (type === 1)     // Element node:
            s += textContent(c); // recurse
    }
    return s;
}
```

Note that the nodeValue property is read/write and you can set it to change the content displayed by a Text node.

Creating, Inserting, and Deleting Nodes

We've seen how to query and alter document content using strings of HTML and plain text. And we've also seen that we can traverse a Document to examine the individual Element and Text nodes that it is made of. It is also possible to alter a document at the level of individual nodes. The Document type defines methods for creating Element and Text objects, and the Node type defines methods for inserting, deleting, and replacing nodes in the tree. The following function demonstrates how to create and insert an element into the document:

```
// Asynchronously load and execute a script
function loadasync(url) {
    // Create a <script> element
    var s = document.createElement("script");
    // Set its src attribute
    s.src = url;
    // Insert the <script> into the <head>
    document.head.appendChild(s);
}
```

As shown above, you can create new Element nodes with the createElement() method of the Document object. Pass the tag name of the element as the method argument.

Text nodes are created with a similar method:

```
var t = document.createTextNode("text node");
```

Another way to create new document nodes is to make copies of existing ones. Every node has a cloneNode() method that returns a new copy of the node. Pass true to recursively copy all descendants as well, or false to only make a shallow copy.

Once you have a new node, you can insert it into the document with the Node methods appendChild() or insertBefore(). appendChild() is invoked on the Element node that you want to insert into, and it inserts the specified node so that it becomes the lastChild of that node.

insertBefore() is like appendChild(), but it takes two arguments. The first argument is the node to be inserted. The second argument is the node before which that node is to be inserted. This method is invoked on the node that will be the parent of the new node, and the second argument must be a child of that parent node. If you pass null as that second argument, the insertBefore() behaves like appendChild() and inserts at the end.

Here is a simple function for inserting a node at a numerical index. The function demonstrates both appendChild() and insertBefore():

```
// Insert the child node into parent at index n
function insertAt(parent, child, n) {
    if (n < 0 || n > parent.childNodes.length)
        throw new Error("invalid index");
    else if (n == parent.childNodes.length)
        parent.appendChild(child);
    else
        parent.insertBefore(child,parent.childNodes[n]);
}
```

If you call appendChild() or insertBefore() to insert a node that is already in the document, that node will automatically be removed from its current position and reinserted at its new position: there is no need to explicitly remove the node.

The removeChild() method removes a node from the document tree. Be careful, however: this method isn't invoked on the node to be removed but (as the "child" part of its name implies) on the parent of that node. Invoke the method on the parent node and pass the child node that is to be removed as the method argument. To remove the node n from the document, you'd write:

```
n.parentNode.removeChild(n);
```

replaceChild() removes one child node and replaces it with a new one. Invoke this method on the parent node, passing the new node as the first argument and the node to be replaced as the second argument. To replace the node n with a string of text, for example, you could write:

```
var t = document.createTextNode("[ REDACTED ]");
n.parentNode.replaceChild(t, n);
```

The following function demonstrates another use of `replace Child()`:

```
// Replace the node n with a new <b> element and
// make n a child of that element.
function embolden(n) {
    // If n is a string treat it as an element id
    if (typeof n == "string")
        n = document.getElementById(n);
    // Create a <b> element
    var b = document.createElement("b");
    // Replace n with the <b> element
    n.parentNode.replaceChild(b, n);
    // Make n a child of the <b> element
    b.appendChild(n);
}
```

Element Style

Cascading Style Sheets (CSS) is a standard for specifying the visual presentation of HTML documents. CSS is intended for use by graphic designers: it allows a designer to precisely specify fonts, colors, margins, indentation, borders, and even the position of document elements. But CSS is also of interest to client-side JavaScript programmers because CSS styles can be scripted. This section explains how to script CSS and assumes that you are already somewhat familiar with CSS.

The most straightforward way to script CSS is to alter the `style` attribute of individual document elements. Like most HTML attributes, `style` is a property of the Element object, and you can manipulate it in JavaScript. The `style` property is unusual, however: its value is not a string or other primitive value but a CSSStyleDeclaration object. The JavaScript properties of this style object represent the CSS properties specified by the HTML `style` attribute. To make the text of an element e big, bold, and blue, for example, you can use the following code to set the JavaScript properties that correspond to the `font-size`, `font-weight`, and `color` style properties:

```
e.style.fontSize = "24pt";
e.style.fontWeight = "bold";
e.style.color = "blue";
```

Many CSS style properties, such as `font-size`, contain hyphens in their names. In JavaScript, a hyphen is interpreted as a minus sign, so it is not possible to write an expression like:

```
e.style.font-size = "24pt"; // Syntax error!
```

Therefore, the names of the properties of the CSSStyleDeclaration object are slightly different from the names of actual CSS properties. If a CSS property name contains one or more hyphens, the CSSStyleDeclaration property name is formed by removing the hyphens and capitalizing the letter immediately following each hyphen. Thus, the CSS property `border-left-width` is accessed through the JavaScript `borderLeftWidth` property. Also, when a CSS property, such as the `float` property, has a name that is a reserved word in JavaScript, that name is prefixed with "css" to create a legal property name.

When working with the style properties of the CSSStyleDeclaration object, remember that all values must be specified as strings. Also, remember that all the positioning properties require units. Thus, it is not correct to set the `left` property like this:

```
// Incorrect: this is a number, not a string
e.style.left = 300;
// Incorrect: the units are missing
e.style.left = "300";
```

Units are required when setting style properties in JavaScript, just as they are when setting style properties in stylesheets. The correct way to set the value of the `left` property of an element e to 300 pixels is:

```
e.style.left = "300px";
```

If you want to set the `left` property to a computed value, be sure to append the units at the end of the computation:

```
e.style.left = (x0 + margin + border + padding) + "px";
```

Notice that the numeric result of the computation will be converted to a string as a side effect of appending the units string.

The **style** attribute of an HTML element is its *inline* style, and it overrides any style specifications in a stylesheet. Inline styles are generally useful for setting style values, and that is what the examples above have all done. You can read the properties of a CSSStyleDeclaration object that represents inline styles, but they return meaningful values only if they've previously been set by your JavaScript code or if the HTML element with which you are working has an inline **style** attribute that sets the desired properties. For example, your document may include a stylesheet that sets the left margin for all paragraphs to 30 pixels, but if you read the **marginLeft** property of one of your paragraph elements, you'll get the empty string unless that paragraph has a **style** attribute that overrides the stylesheet setting.

Sometimes, you may find it easier to set or query the inline style of an element as a single string value rather than as a CSSStyleDeclaration object. To do that, you can use the Element **getAttribute()** and **setAttribute()** methods, or you can use the **cssText** property of the CSSStyleDeclaration object:

```
// Set the style attribute of e to the string s
e.setAttribute("style", s);
e.style.cssText = s;  // Another way to do it

// Query the inline style of the element e
s = e.getAttribute("style");
s = e.style.cssText;  // Another way to do it
```

An alternative to scripting individual CSS styles through the inline **style** property is to script the value of the HTML **class** attribute. Changing an element's **class** changes the set of stylesheet selectors that apply to the element and can cause multiple CSS properties to change at the same time. Suppose, for example, that you want a way to draw the user's attention to individual paragraphs (or other elements) of a document. You might start by defining attention-grabbing styles for any elements that have a class name of "attention":

```css
.attention {   /* Styles to grab the user's attention */
    background-color: yellow;    /* Yellow highlight */
    font-weight: bold;           /* Bold text */
    border: solid black 2px;     /* Black box */
}
```

The identifier `class` is a reserved word in JavaScript, so the HTML `class` attribute is available to JavaScript code using the name `className`. Here is code that sets and clears the `className` property of an element to add and remove the "attention" class for that element:

```javascript
function grabAttention(e) {
    e.className = "attention";
}
function releaseAttention(e) {
    e.className = "";
}
```

HTML elements can be members of more than one CSS class and the `class` attribute holds a space-separated list of class names. The `className` property has a misleading name: `class Names` would have been a much better choice. The functions above assume that the `className` property will specify zero or one class name and do not work when more than one class is in use. If an element already has a class assigned, calling the `grabAttention()` function for that element will overwrite the existing class.

HTML5 addresses this issue by defining a `classList` property for every element. The value of this property is known as a DOMTokenList: a read-only array-like object ("Array-Like Objects" on page 107) whose elements contain the individual class names for the element. More important than its array elements, however, are the methods defined by DOMTokenList. `add()` and `remove()` add and remove individual class names from the element's `class` attribute. `toggle()` adds a classname if it is not already present and removes it otherwise. Finally, the `contains()` method tests whether the `class` attribute contains a specified classname.

Like other DOM collection types, a DOMTokenList is a "live" representation of the element's set of classes, not a static snapshot of the classes at the time the `classList` property is queried. If you obtain a DOMTokenList from the `classList` property of an element and then change the `className` property of that element, those changes are immediately visible through the token list. Similarly, any changes you make through the token list are immediately visible through the `className` property.

Geometry and Scrolling

In this chapter so far we have thought about documents as abstract trees of elements and text nodes. But when a browser renders a document within a window, it creates a visual representation of the document in which each element has a position and a size. Often, web applications can treat documents as trees of elements and never have to think about how those elements are rendered onscreen. Sometimes, however, it is necessary to determine the precise geometry of an element. CSS can be used, for example, to specify the position of an element. If you want to use CSS to dynamically position an element (such as a tooltip or callout) next to some ordinary browser-positioned element, you need to be able to determine the location of that element.

The position of an element is measured in pixels, with the x coordinate increasing to the right and the y coordinate increasing as we go down. There are two different points we can use as the coordinate system origin, however: the x and y coordinates of an element can be relative to the top-left corner of the document or relative to the top-left corner of the *viewport* in which the document is displayed. In top-level windows and tabs, the "viewport" is the portion of the browser that actually displays document content: it excludes browser "chrome" such as menus, toolbars, and tabs. For documents displayed in frames, the viewport is the `<iframe>` element that defines the frame. In either case, when we talk about the position of an element, we must be clear whether we are using document coordinates or viewport coordinates. (Note that viewport co-ordinates are sometimes called window coordinates.)

If the document is smaller than the viewport, or if it has not been scrolled, the upper-left corner of the document is in the upper-left corner of the viewport and the document and view-port coordinate systems are the same. In general, however, to convert between the two coordinate systems, we must add or subtract the *scroll offsets*. If an element has a *y* coordinate of 200 pixels in document coordinates, for example, and if the user has scrolled the browser down by 75 pixels, then that el-ement has a *y* coordinate of 125 pixels in viewport coordinates. Similarly, if an element has an *x* coordinate of 400 in viewport coordinates and the user has scrolled the viewport 200 pixels horizontally, the element's *x* coordinate in document coordi-nates is 600.

Document coordinates are more fundamental than viewport coordinates, and they do not change when the user scrolls. Nevertheless, it is quite common to use viewport coordinates in client-side programming. We use document coordinates when we specify an element position using CSS. But when we query the position of an element we get viewport coordinates. Similarly, when we register handler functions for mouse events, the coordinates of the mouse pointer are reported in viewport coordinates.

In order to convert between coordinate systems, we need to be able to determine the scrollbar positions for the browser win-dow. The `pageXOffset` and `pageYOffset` properties of the Win-dow object provide these values.

It is sometimes useful to be able to determine the viewport size—to find what portions of the document are currently visi-ble, for example. Use the `innerWidth` and `innerHeight` proper-ties of the Window object to query the viewport size.

To determine the size and position of an element, call its `get BoundingClientRect()` method. It expects no arguments and returns an object with properties `left`, `right`, `top`, and `bottom`. The `left` and `top` properties give the *x* and *y* coordinates of the upper-left corner of the element and the **right** and **bottom** properties give the coordinates of the lower-right corner.

This method returns element positions in viewport coordinates. To convert to document coordinates that remain valid even if the user scrolls the browser window, add the scroll offsets:

```
// Get position in viewport coordinates
var box = e.getBoundingClientRect();
// Convert to document coordinates
var x = box.left + window.pageXOffset;
var y = box.top + window.pageYOffset;
```

When an element is displayed in a browser, the element content is surrounded by an optional blank area known as *padding*. The padding is surrounded by an optional border, and the border is surrounded by optional margins. The coordinates returned by **getBoundingClientRect()** include the border and the padding of the element but do not include the element margins.

We saw above that you can query the position of a window's scrollbars with **pageXOffset** and **pageYOffset**. If you want to set the scrollbar position, use the window's **scrollTo()** method. This method takes the *x* and *y* coordinates of a point (in document coordinates) and sets these as the scrollbar offsets. That is, it scrolls the window so that the specified point is in the upper left corner of the viewport. If you specify a point that is too close to the bottom or too close to the right edge of the document, the browser will move it as close as possible to the upper left corner but won't be able to get it all the way there.

The **scrollBy()** method of the Window is similar to **scrollTo()**, but its arguments are relative and are added to the current scrollbar offsets.

Often, instead of scrolling to a numeric location in the document, we just want to scroll so that a certain element in the document is visible. You could compute the position of the element with **getBoundingClientRect()**, convert that position to document coordinates, and then use the **scrollTo()** method, but it is easier to just call the `scrollIntoView()` method on the desired HTML element. This method ensures that the element on which it is invoked is visible in the viewport. By default, it tries to put the top edge of the element at or near the top of the viewport. If you pass `false` as the only argument, it will try to put the bottom edge of the element at the bottom of the viewport. The browser will also scroll the viewport horizontally as needed to make the element visible.

CHAPTER 12

Handling Events

Client-side JavaScript programs use an asynchronous event-driven programming model. In this style of programming, the web browser generates an *event* whenever something interesting happens to the document or browser or to some element or object associated with it. For example, the web browser generates an event when it finishes loading a document, when the user moves the mouse over a hyperlink, or when the user strikes a key on the keyboard. If a JavaScript application cares about a particular type of event, it can register one or more functions to be invoked when events of that type occur.

The *event type* is a string that specifies what kind of event occurred. The type "mousemove," for example, means that the user moved the mouse. The type "keydown" means that a key on the keyboard was pushed down. And the type "load" means that a document (or some other resource) has finished loading from the network. Because the type of an event is just a string, it is sometimes called an *event name*, and indeed, we use this name to identify the specific kind of event we're talking about.

The *event target* is the object on which the event occurred or with which the event is associated. When we speak of an event, we must specify both the type and the target. A load event on a Window, for example, or a click event on a <button> Element. Window, Document, and Element objects are the most common event targets in client-side JavaScript applications, but some events are triggered on other kinds of objects. In Chapter 13 we'll see a readystatechange event that is triggered on an XMLHttpRequest object, for example.

An *event handler* or *event listener* is a function that handles or responds to an event. Applications register their event handler functions with the web browser, specifying an event type and an event target. When an event of the specified type occurs on the specified target, the browser invokes the handler. When event handlers are invoked for an object, we sometimes say that the browser has "fired," "triggered," or "dispatched" the event.

An *event object* is an object that is associated with a particular event and contains details about that event. Event objects are passed as an argument to the event handler function. All event objects have a `type` property that specifies the event type and a `target` property that specifies the event target. Each event type defines a set of properties for its associated event object. The object associated with a mouse event includes the coordinates of the mouse pointer, for example, and the object associated with a keyboard event contains details about the key that was pressed and the modifier keys that were held down. Many event types define only a few standard properties—such as `type` and `target`—and do not carry much other useful information. For those events it is the simple occurrence of the event, not the event details, that matter.

Event propagation is the process by which the browser decides which objects to trigger event handlers on. For events that are specific to a single object (such as the load event on the Window object), no propagation is required. When certain kinds of events occur on document elements, however, they propagate or "bubble" up the document tree. If the user moves the mouse over a hyperlink, the mousemove event is first fired on the `<a>` element that defines that link. Then it is fired on the containing elements: perhaps a `<p>` element, a `<div>` element, and the Document object itself. It is sometimes more convenient to register a single event handler on a Document or other container element than to register handlers on each individual element you're interested in. An event handler can stop the propagation of an event, so that it will not continue to bubble and will not trigger handlers on containing elements.

In another form of event propagation, known as *event capturing*, handlers specially registered on container elements have the opportunity to intercept (or "capture") events before they are delivered to their actual target.

Some events have *default actions* associated with them. When a click event occurs on a hyperlink, for example, the default action is for the browser to follow the link and load a new page. Event handlers can prevent this default action by invoking a method of the event object.

With those terms defined, we can now move on to study events and event handling in detail. The first section that follows is an overview of the many event types supported by web browsers. The next two sections explain how to register event handlers and how the browser invokes those event handlers.

Types of Events

The sections below cover various categories of events: form events, mouse events, key events, and so on. Each section describes the event types in a category, and also explains the important properties of the event objects that are associated with events of those types.

Form Events

Forms and hyperlinks were the first scriptable elements in a web page, way back in the early days of the Web and of JavaScript. This means that form events are some of the most stable and well-supported of all event types. `<form>` elements fire submit events when the form is submitted and reset events when the form is reset. Button-like form elements (including radio buttons and checkboxes) fire click events when the user interacts with them. Form elements that maintain some kind of state generally fire change events when the user changes their state by entering text, selecting an item, or checking a box. For text input fields, a change event is not fired until the user has finished interacting with a form element and has tabbed or clicked to move focus to another element. Form elements respond to keyboard focus changes by firing focus and blur events when they gain and lose the focus.

The submit and reset events have default actions that can be canceled by event handlers, and some click events do, too. The focus and blur events do not bubble, but all the other form events do.

Window Events

Window events represent occurrences related to the browser window itself, rather than any specific document content displayed inside the window. (For some of these events, however, an event with the same name can be fired on document elements.)

The load event is the most important of these events: it is fired when a document and all of its external resources (such as images) are fully loaded and displayed to the user. DOMContentLoaded and readystatechange are alternatives to the load event: they are triggered sooner, when the document and its elements are ready to manipulate, but before external resources are fully loaded.

The unload event is the opposite of load: it is triggered when the user is navigating away from a document. An unload event handler might be used to save the user's state, but it cannot be used to cancel navigation. The beforeunload event is similar to unload but gives you the opportunity to ask the user to confirm that they really want to navigate away from your web page. If a handler for beforeunload returns a string, that string will be displayed to the user in a confirmation dialog before the new page is loaded, and the user will have the opportunity to cancel her navigation and remain at your page.

The focus and blur events described above for form elements are also used as Window events: they are triggered on a window when that browser window receives or loses keyboard focus from the operating system.

Finally, the resize and scroll events are fired on a Window when the user resizes or scrolls the browser window. Scroll events can also be fired on any scrollable document element, such as those with the CSS `overflow` property set.

Mouse Events

Mouse events are generated when the user moves or clicks the mouse over a document. These events are triggered on the most deeply nested element that the mouse pointer is over, but they bubble up through the document. The event object passed to mouse event handlers has properties set that describe the position and button state of the mouse and also specify whether any modifier keys were held down when the event occurred. The `clientX` and `clientY` properties specify the position of the mouse in window coordinates. The `altKey`, `ctrlKey`, `metaKey`, and `shiftKey` properties are set to `true` when the corresponding keyboard modifier keys are held down. And for click events, the `detail` property specifies whether this was a single, double, or triple click.

The mousemove event is triggered any time the user moves or drags the mouse. These events occur frequently, so mousemove handlers must not trigger computationally intensive tasks. The mousedown and mouseup events are triggered when the user presses and releases a mouse button. By registering a mousedown handler that registers a mousemove handler, you can detect and respond to mouse drags. Doing this properly involves being able to capture mouse events so that you continue to receive mousemove events even when the mouse has moved out of the element it started in.

After a mousedown and mouseup event sequence, the browser also triggers a click event. If the user clicks a mouse button twice in a row (within a sufficiently short amount of time), the second click event will be followed by a dblclick event. Browsers often display a context menu when the right mouse button is clicked. They generally fire a contextmenu event before displaying the menu, and if you cancel the event, you can prevent the display of the menu. This is also an easy way to be notified of right mouse button clicks.

When the user moves the mouse so that it goes over a new element, the browser fires a mouseover event on that element. When the mouse moves so that it is no longer over an element, the browser fires a mouseout event on that element. For these events, the event object will have a `relatedTarget` property that specifies the other element involved in the transition. mouseover and mouseout events bubble like all of the mouse events described here. This is often inconvenient, because when a mouseout handler is triggered, you have to check whether the mouse actually left the element you are interested in or if it merely transitioned from one child of the element to another. mouseenter and mouseleave are new, nonbubbling versions of mouseover and mouseout that are supported in new browsers.

When the user rotates the mouse wheel, browsers trigger a mousewheel event. The event object passed with these events includes properties that specify how much, and in which direction, the wheel was rotated.

Key Events

When the web browser has keyboard focus, it generates events each time the user presses or releases a key on the keyboard. Keyboard shortcuts that have meaning to the operating system or to the browser itself are often "eaten" by the OS or browser and may not be visible to JavaScript event handlers, however. Keyboard events are triggered on whatever document element has keyboard focus, and they bubble up to the document and window. If no element has the focus, the events are triggered directly on the document. Keyboard event handlers are passed an event object with a `keyCode` field that specifies what key was pressed or released. In addition to `keyCode`, the event object for key events also has `altKey`, `ctrlKey`, `metaKey`, and `shiftKey` that describe the state of the keyboard modifier keys.

The keydown and keyup events are low-level keyboard events: they are triggered whenever a key (even a modifier key) is pressed or released. When a keydown event generates a printable character, an additional keypress event is triggered after the keydown but before the keyup. (In the case of a key that is held down until it repeats, there may be many keypress events before the keyup event.) The keypress event is a higher-level text event, and its event object specifies the character that was generated, not the key that was pressed. In some browsers (notably Firefox) you must use the `charCode` property of a keypress event object instead of `keyCode`.

The keydown, keyup, and keypress events are supported by all browsers, but there are some interoperability problems because the values of the `keyCode` property are not well standardized.

HTML5 Events

HTML5 and related standards define a host of new APIs for web applications. Many of these APIs define events. This section lists and briefly describes these HTML5 and web application events. Some of these events are ready to be used now; others are not yet widely implemented.

One of the widely advertised features of HTML5 is inclusion of `<audio>` and `<video>` elements for playing sound and video. These elements have a long list of events that they trigger to send notifications about network events, data buffering status, and playback state:

canplay	loadeddata	playing	stalled
canplaythrough	loadedmetadata	progress	suspend
durationchange	loadstart	ratechange	timeupdate
emptied	pause	seeked	volumechange
ended	play	seeking	waiting

These media events are passed an ordinary event object with no special properties. The `target` property identifies the `<audio>` or `<video>` element, however, and that element has many relevant properties and methods.

The HTML5 drag-and-drop API allows JavaScript applications to participate in OS-based drag-and-drop operations, transferring data between web applications and native applications. The API defines the following seven event types:

```
dragstart    drag        dragend
dragenter    dragover    dragleave
drop
```

These drag-and-drop events are triggered with an event object like those sent with mouse events. One additional property, `dataTransfer`, holds a DataTransfer object that contains information about the data being transferred and the formats in which it is available.

HTML5 defines a history management mechanism that allows web applications to interact with the browser's Back and Forward buttons. This mechanism involves events named hashchange and popstate. These events are life cycle notification events like load and unload and are fired at the Window object rather than any individual document element.

HTML5 defines a lot of new features for HTML forms. In addition to standardizing the form input event described earlier, HTML5 also defines a form validation mechanism, which includes an invalid event fired on form elements that have failed validation.

HTML5 includes support for offline web applications that can be installed locally in an application cache so that they can run even when the browser is offline (as when a mobile device is out of network range). The two most important events associated with this are the offline and online events: they are triggered on the Window object whenever the browser loses or gains a network connection. A number of additional events are defined to provide notification of application download progress and application cache updates:

| cached | checking | downloading | error |
| noupdate | obsolete | progress | updateready |

A number of new web application APIs use a message event for asynchronous communication. The Cross-Document Messaging API allows scripts in a document from one server to exchange messages with scripts in a document from another server. This works around the limitations of the same-origin policy ("The Same-Origin Policy" on page 176) in a secure way. Each message that is sent triggers a message event on the Window of the receiving document. The event object passed to the handler includes a `data` property that holds the content of the message as well as `source` and `origin` policies that identify the sender of the message. The message event is used in similar ways for communication with Web Workers and for network communication via Server-Sent Events and WebSockets.

HTML5 and related standards define some events that are triggered on objects other than windows, documents, and document elements. Version 2 of the XMLHttpRequest specification, as well as the File API specification, define a series of events that track the progress of asynchronous I/O. They trigger events on an XMLHttpRequest or FileReader object. Each read operation begins with a loadstart event, followed by progress events and a loadend event. Additionally, each operation ends with a load, error, or abort event just before the final loadend event.

Finally, HTML5 and related standards define a few miscellaneous event types. The Web Storage API defines a storage event (on the Window object) that provides notification of changes to stored data. HTML5 also standardizes the beforeprint and afterprint events that were originally introduced by Microsoft in IE. As their names imply, these events are triggered on a Window immediately before and immediately after its document is printed and provide an opportunity to add or remove content such as the date and time that the document was printed. (These events should not be used to change the presentation of a document for printing because CSS media types already exist for that purpose.)

Touchscreen and Mobile Events

The widespread adoption of mobile devices with touchscreens has required the creation of new categories of events. In many cases, touchscreen events are mapped to traditional event types such as click and scroll. But not every interaction with a touchscreen UI emulates a mouse, and not all touches can be treated as mouse events. This section briefly explains the gesture and touch events generated by Safari when running on Apple's iPhone and iPad devices and also covers the orientationchange event generated when the user rotates the device.

Safari generates gesture events for two-finger scaling and rotation gestures. The gesturestart event is fired when the gesture begins and gestureend is fired when it ends. Between these two events are a sequence of gesturechange events that track the progress of the gesture. The event object sent with these events has numeric `scale` and `rotation` properties. The `scale` property is the ratio of the current distance between the two fingers to the initial distance between the fingers. A "pinch close" gesture has a `scale` less than 1.0, and a "pinch open" gesture has a `scale` greater than 1.0. The `rotation` property is the angle of finger rotation since the start of the event. It is reported in degrees, with positive values indicating clockwise rotation.

Gesture events are high-level events that notify you of a gesture that has already been interpreted. If you want to implement your own custom gestures, you can listen for low-level touch events. When a finger touches the screen, a touchstart event is triggered. When the finger moves, a touchmove event is triggered. And when the finger is lifted from the screen, a touchend event is triggered. Unlike mouse events, touch events do not directly report the coordinates of the touch. Instead, the object sent with a touch event has a `changedTouches` property. This property is an array-like object whose elements each describe the position of a touch.

The orientationchanged event is triggered on the Window object by devices that allow the user to rotate the screen from portrait to landscape mode. The object passed with an orientationchanged event is not useful itself. In mobile Safari, however, the **orientation** property of the Window object gives the current orientation as one of the numbers 0, 90, 180, or –90.

Registering Event Handlers

There are two ways to register event handlers. The first is to set a property on the object or document element that is the event target. The second technique is to pass the handler to a method of the object or element. To complicate matters, there are two versions of each technique. You can set an event handler property in JavaScript code, or for document elements, you can set the corresponding attribute directly in HTML.

Setting Event Handler Properties

The simplest way to register an event handler is by setting a property of the event target to the desired event handler function. By convention, event handler properties have names that consist of the word "on" followed by the event name: **onclick**, **onchange**, **onload**, **onmouseover**, and so on. Note that these property names are case-sensitive and are written in all lowercase, even when the event type (such as "readystatechange" consists of multiple words. Here are two example event handler registrations:

```
// Set the onload property of the Window object.
// The function is the event handler:
// it is invoked when the document loads.
window.onload = function() {
    // Look up a <form> element
    var elt = document.getElementById("address");
    // Register an event handler function that will
    // be invoked right before the form is submitted.
    elt.onsubmit = function() { return validate(this); }
}
```

The shortcoming of event handler properties is that they are designed around the assumption that event targets will have at most one handler for each type of event. If you are writing library code for use in arbitrary documents you can't rely on this technique.

Setting Event Handler Attributes

The event handler properties of a document element can also be set as attributes on the corresponding HTML tag. If you do this, the attribute value should be a string of JavaScript code. That code should be the *body* of the event handler function, not a complete function declaration. That is, your HTML event handler code should not be surrounded by curly braces and prefixed with the `function` keyword. For example:

```
<button onclick="alert('Thank you');">
  Click Here
</button>
```

If an HTML event handler attribute contains multiple Java-Script statements, you must remember to separate those statements with semicolons or to break the attribute value across multiple lines.

Some event types are directed at the browser as a whole, rather than at any particular document element. In JavaScript, handlers for these events are registered on the Window object. In HTML, we place them on the `<body>` tag, but the browser registers them on the Window. The following is the complete list of such event handlers as defined by the draft HTML5 specification:

onafterprint	onfocus	ononline	onresize
onbeforeprint	onhashchange	onpagehide	onstorage
onbeforeunload	onload	onpageshow	onundo
onblur	onmessage	onpopstate	onunload
onerror	onoffline	onredo	

When you specify a string of JavaScript code as the value of an HTML event handler attribute, the browser converts your string into a function that looks something like this:

```
function(event) {
    with(document) {
        with(this.form || {}) {
            with(this) {
```

```
                    /* your code here */
                }
            }
        }
    }
```

We'll see more about the **event** argument and the **with** statements above when we consider event handler invocation in "Event Handler Invocation" on page 218.

addEventListener()

Any object that can be an event target—this includes the Window and Document objects and all document Elements—defines a method named **addEventListener()** that you can use to register an event handler for that target. **addEventListener()** takes three arguments. The first is the event type for which the handler is being registered. The event type (or name) is a string and it should not include the "on" prefix that is used when setting event handler properties. The second argument to **addEventListener()** is the function that should be invoked when the specified type of event occurs. The final argument to **addEventListener()** is an optional boolean value. Normally, you'll pass **false** for this argument or omit it. If you pass **true** instead, your function is registered as a *capturing* event handler and is invoked at a different phase of event dispatch. We will cover event capturing in "Event Propagation" on page 221.

The code below registers two handlers for the click event on a **<button>** element. Note the differences between the two techniques used:

```
<button id="mybutton">Click me</button>
<script>
var b = document.getElementById("mybutton");
b.onclick = function() { alert("Thanks!"); };
b.addEventListener("click",
        function() { alert("Thanks again!"); });
</script>
```

Calling `addEventListener()` with "click" as its first argument does not affect the value of the `onclick` property. In the code above, a button click will generate two `alert()` dialog boxes. More importantly, you can call `addEventListener()` multiple times to register more than one handler function for the same event type on the same object. When an event occurs on an object, all of the handlers registered for that type of event are invoked, in the order in which they were registered. Invoking `addEventListener()` more than once on the same object with the same arguments has no effect—the handler function remains registered only once, and the repeated invocation does not alter the order in which handlers are invoked.

`addEventListener()` is paired with a `removeEventListener()` method that expects the same three arguments but removes an event handler function from an object rather than adding it. It is often useful to temporarily register an event handler and then remove it soon afterward. For example, when you get a mouse-down event, you might register temporary capturing event handlers for mousemove and mouseup events so that you can see if the user drags the mouse. You'd then deregister these handlers when the mouseup event arrives. In such a situation, your event handler removal code might look like this:

```
document.removeEventListener("mousemove",
                             handleMove, true);
document.removeEventListener("mouseup",
                             handleUp, true);
```

Event Handler Invocation

Once you've registered an event handler, the web browser will invoke it automatically when an event of the specified type occurs on the specified object. This section describes event handler invocation in detail, explaining event handler arguments, the invocation context (the `this` value), the invocation scope, and the meaning of the return value of an event handler.

In addition to describing how individual handlers are invoked, this section also explains how events *propagate*: how a single event can trigger the invocation of multiple handlers on the original event target and also on containing elements of the document.

Event Handler Argument

Event handlers are invoked with an event object as their single argument. The properties of the event object (described earlier in this chapter) provide details about the event.

Recall from "Setting Event Handler Attributes" on page 216 that when you register an event handler by setting an HTML attribute, the browser converts your string of JavaScript code into a function with a single argument named `event`. This means that HTML event handlers can refer to the event object as `event`.

Event Handler Context

When you register an event handler by setting a property, it looks as if you are defining a new method on an object:

```
e.onclick = function() { /* handler code */ };
```

It isn't surprising, therefore, that event handlers are invoked as methods of the object on which they are defined. That is, within the body of an event handler, the `this` keyword refers to the event target.

Handlers registered using `addEventListener()` are also invoked with the target as their `this` value.

Event Handler Scope

Like all JavaScript functions, event handlers are lexically scoped. They are executed in the scope in which they are defined, not the scope from which they are invoked, and they can access any local variables from that scope.

Event handlers registered as HTML attributes are a special case, however. They are converted into top-level functions that have access to global variables but not to any local variables. But, for historical reasons, they run with a modified scope chain. Event handlers defined by HTML attributes can use the properties of the target object, the containing <form> object (if there is one), and the Document object as if they are local variables. "Setting Event Handler Attributes" on page 216 shows how an event handler function is created from an HTML event handler attribute, and the code there approximates this modified scope chain using `with` statements.

HTML attributes are not natural places to include long strings of code, and this modified scope chain allows helpful shortcuts. You can use `tagName` instead of `this.tagName`. You can use `getElementById` instead of `document.getElementById`. And, for document elements that are inside a <form>, you can refer to any other form element by ID, using `zipcode`, for example, instead of `this.form.zipcode`.

On the other hand, the modified scope chain of HTML event handlers is a source of pitfalls, since the properties of each of the objects in the chain shadow any properties of the same name in the global object. This is a particular problem with forms, because the names and IDs of form elements define properties on the containing form element. So if a form contains an element with the ID "location," for example, all HTML event handlers within that form must use `window.location` instead of `location` if they want to refer to the window's Location object.

Handler Return Value

The return value of an event handler registered by setting an object property or an HTML attribute is sometimes significant. In general, a return value of `false` tells the browser that it should not perform the default action associated with the event. The `onclick` handler of a Submit button in a form, for example, can return `false` to prevent the browser from submitting the form. (This is useful if the user's input fails client-side validation.) Similarly, an `onkeypress` handler on an input field can filter keyboard input by returning `false` if the user types an inappropriate character.

The return value of the `onbeforeunload` handler of the Window object is also significant. This event is triggered when the browser is about to navigate to a new page. If this event handler returns a string, it will be displayed in a modal dialog box that asks the user to confirm that she wants to leave the page.

It is important to understand that event handler return values are significant only for handlers registered as properties. We'll see below that event handlers registered with `addEventListener()` must instead call the `preventDefault()` method of the event object.

Event Propagation

When the target of an event is the Window object, or some other standalone object (such as an XMLHttpRequest), the browser responds to an event simply by invoking the appropriate handlers on that one object. When the event target is a Document or document Element, however, the situation is more complicated.

After the event handlers registered on the target element are invoked, most events "bubble" up the DOM tree. The event handlers of the target's parent are invoked. Then the handlers registered on the target's grandparent are invoked. This continues up to the Document object, and then beyond to the Window object. Event bubbling provides an alternative to registering handlers on lots of individual document elements: instead you can register a single handler on a common ancestor element and handle events there. You might register a "change" handler on a `<form>` element, for example, instead of registering a "change" handler for every element in the form.

Most events that occur on document elements bubble. Notable exceptions are the focus, blur, and scroll events. The load event on document elements bubbles, but it stops bubbling at the Document object and does not propagate on to the Window object. The load event of the Window object is triggered only when the entire document has loaded.

Event bubbling is the third "phase" of event propagation. The invocation of the event handlers of the target object itself is the second phase. The first phase, which occurs even before the target handlers are invoked, is called the "capturing" phase. Recall that `addEventListener()` takes a boolean value as its third argument. If that argument is `true`, the event handler is registered as a capturing event handler for invocation during this first phase of event propagation.

The capturing phase of event propagation is like the bubbling phase in reverse. The capturing handlers of the Window object are invoked first, then the capturing handlers of the Document object, then of the body object, and so on down the DOM tree until the capturing event handlers of the parent of the event target are invoked. Capturing event handlers registered on the event target itself are not invoked.

Event capturing provides an opportunity to peek at events before they are delivered to their target. A capturing event handler can be used for debugging, or it can be used along with the event cancellation technique described below to filter events so that the target event handlers are never actually invoked. One common use for event capturing is handling mouse drags, where mouse motion events need to be handled by the object being dragged, not the document elements over which it is dragged.

Event Cancellation

"Handler Return Value" on page 220 explained that the return value of event handlers registered as properties can be used to cancel the browser's default action for the event. You can also cancel the default action for an event by invoking the `prevent Default()` method of the event object.

Canceling the default action associated with an event is only one kind of event cancellation. We can also cancel the propagation of events. Event objects have a `stopPropaga tion()` method that you can invoke to prevent the continued propagation of the event. If there are other handlers defined on the same object, the rest of those handlers will still be invoked, but no event handlers on any other object will be invoked after `stopPropagation()` is called. The `stop Propagation()` method can be called at any time during event propagation. It works during the capturing phase, at the event target itself, and during the bubbling phase. Another method on the Event object, named `stopImmediatePropagation()`, prevents the propagation of the event to any other objects and also prevents the invocation of any other event handlers registered on the same object.

CHAPTER 13

Networking

This chapter describes four techniques for client-side Java-Script networking. The first, `XMLHttpRequest`, is well-known and widely-used in the "Ajax" application architecture. This API is by far the most important of the four, and the bulk of the chapter is devoted to it. The chapter also demonstrates the JSONP technique for Ajax-style networking with the `<script>` tag, as well as "server push" or "Comet" style networking with the new EventSource API, and bidirectional socket-style networking with WebSockets.

Using XMLHttpRequest

Browsers define their HTTP API on an XMLHttpRequest class. Each instance of this class represents a single HTTP request/response pair, and the properties and methods of the object allow you to specify request details and extract response data. XMLHttpRequest is often abbreviated as XHR, and this chapter uses the term XHR2 to refer to cutting-edge features introduced by drafts of version 2 of the XHR specification. Note that the XMLHttpRequest API has nothing to do with XML: the name is a historical accident that we're simply stuck with.

The first step in using the XHR API, of course, is to instantiate an XMLHttpRequest object:

```
var request = new XMLHttpRequest();
```

You can also reuse an existing XMLHttpRequest object, but note that doing so will abort any request pending through that object.

Any HTTP request consists of four parts:

- the HTTP request method or "verb"
- the URL being requested
- an optional set of request headers, which may include authentication information
- an optional request body

The HTTP response sent by a server has three parts:

- a numeric and textual status code that indicates the success or failure of the request
- a set of response headers
- the response body

The first two subsections below demonstrate how to set each of the parts of an HTTP request and how to query each of the parts of an HTTP response with the XHR API. Those key sections are followed by coverage of more specialized topics.

XMLHttpRequest and Local Files

The ability to use relative URLs in web pages usually means that we can develop and test our HTML using the local file system and then deploy it unchanged to a web server. This is generally not possible when doing Ajax programming with XMLHttpRequest, however. XMLHttpRequest is designed to work with the HTTP and HTTPS protocols, not the file:// protocol. This means that when working with XMLHttpRequest, you generally have to upload your files to a web server (or run a server locally) in order to test them.

The basic request/response architecture of HTTP is pretty simple and easy to work with. In practice, however, there are all sorts of complications: clients and server exchange cookies, servers redirect browsers to other servers, some resources are cached and others are not, some clients send all their requests through proxy servers, and so on. XMLHttpRequest is not a protocol-level HTTP API but instead a browser-level API. The browser takes care of cookies, redirects, caching, and proxies and your code need worry only about requests and responses.

Specifying the Request

After creating an XMLHttpRequest object, the next step in making an HTTP request is to call the open() method of your XMLHttpRequest object to specify the two required parts of the request, the method and the URL:

```
request.open("GET",        // Begin a HTTP GET request
             "data.csv"); // For the contents of this URL
```

The first argument to open() specifies the HTTP method or verb. The "GET" and "POST" methods are universally supported. "GET" is used for most "regular" requests, and it is appropriate when the URL completely specifies the requested resource, when the request has no side effects on the server, and when the server's response is cacheable. The "POST" method includes additional data in the request body and that data is often stored in a database on the server (a side effect).

In addition to "GET" and "POST", the XMLHttpRequest specification also allows "DELETE," "HEAD," "OPTIONS," and "PUT" as the first argument to open().

The second argument to open() is the URL that is the subject of the request. This is relative to the URL of the document that contains the script that is calling open(). If you specify an absolute URL, the protocol, host, and port must generally match those of the containing document: cross-origin HTTP requests normally cause an error. (But the XHR2 allows cross-origin requests when the server explicitly allows it; see "Cross-Origin HTTP Requests" on page 232.)

The next step in the request process is to set the request headers, if any. "POST" requests, for example, need a "Content-Type" header to specify the MIME type of the request body:

```
request.setRequestHeader("Content-Type", "text/plain");
```

If you call setRequestHeader() multiple times for the same header, the new value does not replace the previously specified value: instead, the HTTP request will include multiple copies of the header or the header will specify multiple values.

You cannot specify the "Content-Length," "Date," "Referer," or "User-Agent" headers yourself: XMLHttpRequest will add those automatically for you and will not allow you to spoof them. Similarly, XMLHttpRequest object automatically handles cookies, and connection lifetime, charset, and encoding negotiations, so you're not allowed to set any of those headers either.

The final step in making an HTTP request with XMLHttpRequest is to specify the optional request body and send it off to the server. Do this with the send() method:

```
request.send(null);
```

GET requests never have a body, so you should pass null or omit the argument. POST requests do generally have a body, and it should match the "Content-Type" header you specified with setRequestHeader().

Example 13-1 uses each of the XMLHttpRequest methods we've described so far. It POSTs a string of text to a server and ignores any response the server sends. Note that the string sent in the request body may be a complex one: it might be a JavaScript object encoded with JSON.stringify() or a form-encoded set of name/value pairs.

Example 13-1. POSTing plain text to a server

```
function postMessage(msg) {
    var r = new XMLHttpRequest(); // New request
    r.open("POST", "/log.php");   // POST to this URL
    // Specify that the request body is UTF8 text
    r.setRequestHeader("Content-Type",
```

```
                    "text/plain;charset=UTF-8");
    // Send msg as the request body
    r.send(msg);
    // Ignore any response or any error.
}
```

Note that the send() method in Example 13-1 initiates the request and then returns: it does not block while waiting for the server's response. HTTP responses are asynchronous, as demonstrated in the following section.

Retrieving the Response

A complete HTTP response consists of a status code, a set of response headers, and a response body. These are available through properties and methods of the XMLHttpRequest object:

- The status and statusText properties return the HTTP status in numeric and textual forms. These properties hold standard HTTP values like 200 and "OK" for successful requests, and 404 and "Not Found" for URLs that don't match any resource on the server.

- The response headers can be queried with getResponse Header() and getAllResponseHeaders().

- The response body is available in textual form from the responseText property.

The XMLHttpRequest object is used asynchronously: the send() method returns immediately after sending the request, and the response methods and properties listed above aren't valid until the response is received. To be notified when the response is ready, you must listen for readystatechange events (or the new XHR2 progress events described in "HTTP Progress Events" on page 231) on the XMLHttpRequest object. But to understand this event type, you must first understand the readyState property.

readyState is an integer that specifies the status of an HTTP request, and its possible values are the following:

Value	Meaning
0	open() has not been called yet
1	open() has been called
2	Headers have been received
3	The response body is being received
4	The response is complete

To listen for readystatechange events, set the onreadystate change property of the XMLHttpRequest object to your event handler function. (Or call addEventListener()). Example 13-2 defines a getText() function that demonstrates how to listen for readystatechange events. The event handler first ensures that the request is complete. If so, it checks the response status code to ensure that the request was successful. Then it looks at the "Content-Type" header to verify that the response was of the expected type. If all three conditions are satisfied, it passes the response body (as text) to a specified callback function. That callback could then process the response further, by passing it to JSON.parse(), for example.

Example 13-2. Getting an HTTP response onreadystatechange

```
// Issue an HTTP GET request for the specified URL.
// When the response arrives successfully, verify
// that it is plain text and if so, pass it the text
// to the specified callback function
function getText(url, callback) {
    var r = new XMLHttpRequest(); // New request
    r.open("GET", url);           // Specify URL
    r.onreadystatechange = function() {
        // If the request is compete and was successful
        if (r.readyState === 4 && r.status === 200) {
            var type = r.getResponseHeader("Content-Type");
            // If response is text, pass it to callback
            if (type.match(/^text/))
                callback(r.responseText);
        }
    };
    r.send(null);                 // Send the request!
}
```

HTTP Progress Events

In the examples above, we've used the readystatechange event to detect the completion of an HTTP request. The XHR2 draft specification defines a more useful set of events. In this new event model, the XMLHttpRequest object triggers different types of events at different phases of the request so that it is no longer necessary to check the readyState property.

In browsers that support them, these new events are triggered as follows. When the send() method is called, a single loadstart event is fired. While the server's response is being downloaded, the XMLHttpRequest object fires progress events, typically every 50 milliseconds or so, and you can use these events to give the user feedback about the progress of the request. If a request completes very quickly, it may never fire a progress event. When a request is complete, a load event is fired.

A complete request is not necessarily a successful request, and your handler for the load event should check the status code of the XMLHttpRequest object to ensure that you received an HTTP "200 OK" response rather than a "404 Not Found" response, for example.

There are three ways that an HTTP request can fail to complete, and three corresponding events. If a request times out, the timeout event is triggered. If a request is aborted, the abort event is triggered. Finally, other network errors, such as too many redirects, can prevent the completion of a request, and the error event is triggered when this happens.

The event object associated with these progress events has three useful properties in addition to the normal Event object properties like type and timestamp. The loaded property is the number of bytes that have been transferred so far. The total property is the total length (in bytes) of the data to be transferred, from the "Content-Length" header, or 0 if the content length is not known. Finally, the lengthComputable property is true if the content length is known and is false otherwise.

Obviously, the `total` and `loaded` properties are particularly useful in progress event handlers:

```
request.onprogress = function(e) {
    if (e.lengthComputable) {
        var p = Math.round(100*e.loaded/e.total);
        progress.innerHTML = p + "% Complete";
    }
}
```

In addition to defining these useful events for monitoring the download of an HTTP response, XHR2 also allows the events to be used to monitor the upload of an HTTP request. In browsers that have implemented this feature, the XMLHttpRequest object will have an `upload` property. The value of the `upload` property is an object that defines an `addEventListener()` method and defines a full set of progress event properties, such as `onprogress` and `onload`.

You can use the upload event handlers just as you would use the regular progress event handlers. For an XMLHttpRequest object x, set `x.onprogress` to monitor the download progress of the response. And set `x.upload.onprogress` to monitor the upload progress of the request.

Cross-Origin HTTP Requests

As part of the same-origin security policy ("The Same-Origin Policy" on page 176), the XMLHttpRequest object can normally issue HTTP requests only to the server from which the document that uses it was downloaded. This restriction closes security holes, but it is heavy-handed and also prevents a number of legitimate uses for cross-origin requests. You can use cross-origin URLs with `<form>` and `<iframe>` elements, and the browser will display the resulting cross-origin document. But because of the same-origin policy, the browser won't allow the original script to inspect the contents of the cross-origin document. With XMLHttpRequest, document contents are always exposed through the `responseText` property, so the same-origin policy cannot allow XMLHttpRequest to make cross-origin requests. (Note that the `<script>` element has never really been subject to the same-origin policy: it will download and execute any script, regardless of origin. As we'll see in "HTTP by <script>: JSONP" on page 233, this freedom to make cross-origin requests makes the <script> element an attractive Ajax transport alternative to XMLHttpRequest.)

XHR2 allows cross-origin requests to websites that opt-in by sending appropriate CORS (Cross-Origin Resource Sharing) headers in their HTTP responses. As a web programmer, there is nothing special you need to do to make this work: if the browser supports CORS for XMLHttpRequest and if the website you are trying to make a cross-origin request to has decided to allow cross-origin requests with CORS, the same-origin policy will be relaxed and your cross-origin requests will just work.

HTTP by <script>: JSONP

For certain kinds of content, a <script> element can be used as a useful alternative to XMLHttpRequest. Simply set the src attribute of a <script> (and insert it into the document if it isn't already there) and the browser will generate an HTTP request to download the URL you specify. <script> elements are useful Ajax transports for one primary reason: they are not subject to the same-origin policy, so you can use them to request data from servers other than your own.

The technique of using a <script> element as an Ajax transport has come to be known as JSONP: it works when the response body of the HTTP request is JSON-encoded. The "P" stands for "padding" or "prefix"—this will be explained in a moment.

Suppose you've written a service that handles GET requests and returns JSON-encoded data. Same-origin documents can use it with XMLHttpRequest and JSON.parse(). If you enable CORS on your server, cross-origin documents in new browsers can also use your service with XMLHttpRequest. Cross-origin documents in older browsers that do not support CORS can only access your service with a <script> element, however. Your JSON response body is (by definition) valid JavaScript code, and the browser will execute it when it arrives. Executing JSON-encoded data decodes it, but the result is still just data, and it doesn't *do* anything.

This is where the P part of JSONP comes in. When invoked through a `<script>` element, your service must "pad" its response by surrounding it with parentheses and prefixing it with the name of a JavaScript function. Instead of just sending JSON data like this:

```
[1, 2, {"buckle": "my shoe"}]
```

It sends a padded-JSON response like this:

```
handleResponse(
[1, 2, {"buckle": "my shoe"}]
)
```

As the body of a `<script>` element, this padded response does something valuable: it evaluates the JSON-encoded data (which is nothing more than one big JavaScript expression, after all) and then passes it to the function `handleResponse()`, which, we assume, the containing document has defined to do something useful with the data.

In order for this to work, we have to have some way to tell the service that it is being invoked from a `<script>` element and must send a JSONP response instead of a plain JSON response. This can be done by adding a query parameter to the URL: appending `?json` (or `&json`), for example.

In practice, services that support JSONP do not dictate a function name like "handleResponse" that all clients must implement. Instead, they use the value of a query parameter to allow the client to specify a function name, and then use that function name as the padding in the response. Example 13-3 uses a query parameter named "jsonp" to specify the name of the callback function.

Example 13-3 defines a function `getJSONP()` that makes a JSONP request. This example is a little tricky, and there are some things you should note about it. First, notice how it creates a new `<script>` element, sets its URL, and inserts it into the document. It is this insertion that triggers the HTTP request. Second, notice that the example creates a new internal callback function for each request, storing the function as a property of getJSONP() itself. Finally, note that callback performs some necessary cleanup: it removes the script element and deletes itself.

Example 13-3. Making a JSONP request with a script element

```
// Make a JSONP request to the specified URL and
// pass the parsed response data to the specified
// callback. Add a query parameter named "jsonp" to
// the URL to specify the name of the callback
// function for the request.
function getJSONP(url, callback) {
    // Create a unique callback name for this request
    // The name will be a property of this function.
    var cbnum = "cb" + getJSONP.counter++;
    var cbname = "getJSONP." + cbnum;

    // Add the callback name to the url query string.
    if (url.indexOf("?") === -1)
        url += "?jsonp=" + cbname;
    else
        url += "&jsonp=" + cbname;

    // Create the script element for this request
    var script = document.createElement("script");

    // Define the callback function that we named above.
    getJSONP[cbnum] = function(response) {
        try {
            callback(response); // Handle the response
        }
        finally { // Always clean up, even on error
            delete getJSONP[cbnum];
            script.parentNode.removeChild(script);
        }
    };

    // Now trigger the HTTP request
    script.src = url;
    document.body.appendChild(script);
}
```

```
// The counter used to assign callback names
getJSONP.counter = 0;
```

Scripts and Security

In order to use a `<script>` element as an Ajax transport, you
have to allow your web page to run whatever JavaScript code
the remote server chooses to send you. This means that you
must not use the technique described here with untrusted
servers. And when you do use it with trusted servers, keep in
mind that if an attacker can hack into that server, then the
hacker can take over your web page, run any code she wants
and display any content she wants, and that content will appear to come from your site.

With that said, note that it has become commonplace for websites to use trusted third-party scripts, especially to embed
advertising or "widgets" into a page. Using a `<script>` as an
Ajax transport to communicate with a trusted web service is
no more dangerous than that.

Server-Sent Events

In normal HTTP networking with XHR or the `<script>` tag,
the client requests or "pulls" data from the server when it needs
it. There is another style of HTTP-based networking that is
used by some web applications. In "server push" or "comet,"
the client and server establish an HTTP connection, but leave
it open indefinitely, which allows the server to push data to the
client through that open connection.

It is possible but difficult to implement this style of networking
with XHR, but a new HTML5-related standard known as
Server-Sent Events defines a simple EventSource API that
makes it trivial to receive and respond to messages pushed by
the server. To use Server-Sent Events, simply pass a URL to the
`EventSource()` constructor and then listen for message events
on the returned object:

```
var ticker = new EventSource("stockprices.php");
ticker.onmessage = function(e) {
    var type = e.type;
    var data = e.data;

    // Now process the event type and event data strings.
}
```

The event object associated with a message event has a **data** property that holds whatever string the server sent as the payload for this event. The event object also has a **type** property like all event objects do. The default value is "message," but the event source can specify a different string for the property. A single **onmessage** event handler receives all events from a given server event source, and can dispatch them, if necessary, based on their **type** property.

The Server-Sent Event protocol is straightforward. The client initiates a connection to the server (when it creates the **EventSource** object) and the server keeps this connection open. When an event occurs, the server writes lines of text to the connection. An event going over the wire might look like this:

```
event: bid    event type
data: GOOG    sets the data property
data: 999     appends newline and more data
              blank line triggers the event
```

WebSockets

All of the networking APIs described so far in this chapter are HTTP-based, which means that they are all constrained by the fundamental nature of the HTTP: it is a stateless protocol that consists of client requests and server responses. HTTP is actually a specialized network protocol. More general network protocols often involve longer-lived connections and bidirectional message exchange over TCP sockets. It is not safe to give untrusted client-side JavaScript code access to low-level TCP sockets, but the WebSocket API defines a secure alternative: it allows client-side code to create bidirectional socket-type connections to servers that support the WebSocket protocol. This makes it much easier to perform certain kinds of networking tasks.

The WebSocket API is surprisingly easy to use. First, create a socket with the WebSocket() constructor:

```
var s = new WebSocket("ws://ws.example.com/resource");
```

The argument to the WebSocket() constructor is a URL that uses the ws:// protocol (or wss:// for a secure connection like that used by https://). The URL specifies the host to connect to, and may also specify a port (WebSockets use the same default ports as HTTP and HTTPS) and a path or resource.

Once you have created a socket, you generally register event handlers on it:

```
s.onopen = function(e) {  /* The socket is open. */ };
s.onclose = function(e) { /* The socket closed. */ };
s.onerror = function(e) { /* Something went wrong! */ };
s.onmessage = function(e) {
    var m = e.data;  /* The server sent a message. */
};
```

In order to send data to the server over the socket, you call the send() method of the socket:

```
s.send("Hello, server!");
```

When your code is done communicating with the server, you can close a WebSocket by calling its close() method.

WebSocket communication is completely bidirectional. Once a WebSocket connection has been established, the client and server can send messages to each other at any time, and that communication does not have to take the form of requests and responses.

CHAPTER 14

Client-Side Storage

Web applications can use browser APIs to store data locally on the user's computer. This client-side storage serves to give the web browser a memory. Web apps can store user preferences, for example, or even store their complete state, so that they can resume exactly where you left off at the end of your last visit. Client-side storage is segregated by origin, so pages from one site can't read the data stored by pages from another site. But two pages from the same site can share storage and can use it as a communication mechanism. Data input in a form on one page can be displayed in a table on another page, for example. Web applications can choose the lifetime of the data they store: data can be stored temporarily so that it is retained only until the window closes or the browser exits, or it can be saved to the hard drive and stored permanently, so that it is available months or years later. This chapter covers two forms of client-side storage: the modern Web Storage API and the ancient Cookies API.

Storage, Security, and Privacy

Web browsers often offer to remember web passwords for you, and they store them safely in encrypted form on the disk. But none of the forms of client-side data storage described in this chapter involve encryption: anything you save resides on the user's hard disk in unencrypted form. Stored data is therefore accessible to curious users who share access to the computer and to malicious software (such as spyware) that exists on the computer. For this reason, no form of client-side storage should ever be used for passwords, financial account numbers, or other similarly sensitive information.

Also, bear in mind that many web users mistrust websites that use cookies or other client-side storage mechanisms to do anything that resembles "tracking." Try to use the storage mechanisms discussed in this chapter to enhance a user's experience at your site; don't use them as a privacy-invading data collection mechanism. If too many sites abuse client-side storage, users will disable it or clear it frequently, which will defeat the purpose and cripple the sites that depend on it.

localStorage and sessionStorage

Browsers that implement the "Web Storage" draft specification define two properties on the Window object: `localStorage` and `sessionStorage`. Both properties refer to a Storage object—a persistent associative array that maps string keys to string values. Storage objects work much like regular JavaScript objects: simply set a property of the object to a string, and the browser will store that string for you. The difference between `localStorage` and `sessionStorage` has to do with *lifetime* and *scope*: how long the data is saved for and who the data is accessible to.

Storage lifetime and scope are explained in more detail below. First, however, let's look at some examples. The following code uses `localStorage`, but it would also work with `sessionStorage`:

```
// Query a stored value.
var name = localStorage.username;
// The array notation equivalent
name = localStorage["username"];
if (!name) { // If no name stored, get one and store it
    name = prompt("What is your name?");
    localStorage.username = name;
```

```
    }

    // Iterate through all stored name/value pairs
    for(var key in localStorage) {
        var value = localStorage[key];
    }
```

Storage objects also define methods for storing, retrieving, iterating, and deleting data. Those methods are covered in "Storage API" on page 243.

The Web Storage draft specification says that we should be able to store structured data (objects and arrays) as well as primitive values and built-in types such as dates, regular expressions, and even File objects. At the time of this writing, however, browsers only allow the storage of strings. If you want to store and retrieve other kinds of data, you'll have to encode and decode it yourself. For example:

```
    // Stored numbers are automatically converted to strings.
    // You must parse it when retrieving it from storage.
    localStorage.x = 10;
    var x = parseInt(localStorage.x);

    // Convert a Date to a string when setting it.
    localStorage.lastRead = (new Date()).toUTCString();
    // And parse it when getting.
    var last = new Date(Date.parse(localStorage.lastRead));

    // Use JSON to stringify and parse objects and arrays.
    localStorage.data = JSON.stringify(data);
    var data = JSON.parse(localStorage.data);
```

Storage Lifetime and Scope

The difference between localStorage and sessionStorage involves the lifetime and scope of the storage. Data stored through localStorage is permanent: it does not expire and remains stored on the user's computer until a web app deletes it or the user asks the browser (through some browser-specific UI) to delete it.

localStorage is scoped to the document origin. As explained in "The Same-Origin Policy" on page 176, the origin of a document is defined by its protocol, hostname, and port, so each of the following URLs has a different origin:

```
http://www.example.com
https://www.example.com        // Different protocol
http://static.example.com      // Different hostname
http://www.example.com:8000    // Different port
```

All documents with the same origin share the same `localStorage` data (regardless of the origin of the scripts that actually access `localStorage`). They can read each other's data. And they can overwrite each other's data. But documents with different origins can never read or overwrite each other's data (even if they're both running a script from the same third-party server).

Note that `localStorage` is also scoped by browser vendor. If you visit a site using Firefox, and then visit again using Chrome (for example), any data stored during the first visit will not be accessible during the second visit.

Data stored through `sessionStorage` has a different lifetime than data stored through `localStorage`: it has the same lifetime as the top-level window or browser tab in which the script that stored it is running. When the window or tab is permanently closed, any data stored through `sessionStorage` is deleted. (Note, however, that modern browsers have the ability to re-open recently closed tabs and restore the last browsing session, so the lifetime of these tabs and their associated `sessionStorage` may be longer than it seems.)

Like `localStorage`, `sessionStorage` is scoped to the document origin so that documents with different origins will never share `sessionStorage`. But `sessionStorage` is also scoped on a per-window basis. If a user has two browser tabs displaying documents from the same origin, those two tabs have separate `sessionStorage` data: the scripts running in one tab cannot read or overwrite the data written by scripts in the other tab, even if both tabs are visiting exactly the same page and are running exactly the same scripts.

Note that this window-based scoping of `sessionStorage` is only for top-level windows. If one browser tab contains two `<iframe>` elements, and those frames hold two documents with the same origin, those two framed documents will share `sessionStorage`.

Storage API

`localStorage` and `sessionStorage` are often used as if they were regular JavaScript objects: set a property to store a string and query the property to retrieve it. But these objects also define a more formal method-based API. To store a value, pass the name and value to `setItem()`. To retrieve a value, pass the name to `getItem()`. To delete a value, pass the name to `removeItem()`. (In most browsers you can also use the `delete` operator to remove a value, just as you would for an ordinary object, but this technique does not work in IE8.) To delete all stored values, call `clear()` (with no arguments). Finally, to enumerate the names of all stored values, use the `length` property and pass numbers from 0 to `length`–1 to the `key()` method. Here are some examples using `localStorage`. The same code would work using `sessionStorage` instead:

```
localStorage.setItem("x", 1); // Store an item "x"
localStorage.getItem("x");    // Retrieve its value

// Enumerate all stored name/value pairs
// Length gives the # of pairs
for(var i = 0; i < localStorage.length; i++) {
    // Get the name of pair i
    var name = localStorage.key(i);
    // Get the value of that pair
    var value = localStorage.getItem(name);
}

localStorage.removeItem("x"); // Delete the item "x"
localStorage.clear(); // Delete any other items, too
```

Storage Events

Whenever the data stored in `localStorage` or `sessionStorage` changes, the browser triggers a storage event on any other Window objects to which that data is visible (but not on the window that made the change). If a browser has two tabs open to pages with the same origin, and one of those pages stores a value in `localStorage`, the other tab will receive a storage event. Remember that `sessionStorage` is scoped to the top-level window, so storage events are only triggered for `sessionStorage` changes when there are frames involved. Also note that storage events are only triggered when storage actually changes. Setting an existing stored item to its current value does not trigger an event, nor does removing an item that does not exist in storage.

Register a handler for storage events with `addEventListener()` (or `attachEvent()` in IE). In most browsers, you can also set the `onstorage` property of the Window object, but at the time of this writing, Firefox does not support that property.

The event object associated with a storage event has five important properties (they are not supported by IE8, unfortunately):

key
> The name or key of the item that was set or removed. If the `clear()` method was called, this property will be `null`.

newValue
> Holds the new value of the item, or `null` if `removeItem()` was called.

oldValue
> Holds the old value of an existing item that changed or was deleted, or `null` if a new item was inserted.

storageArea
> This property will equal either the `localStorage` or the `sessionStorage` property of the target Window object.

```
url
```
    The URL (as a string) of the document whose script made
    this storage change.

Finally, note that `localStorage` and the storage event can serve
as a broadcast mechanism by which a browser sends a message
to all windows that are currently visiting the same website. If
a user requests that a website stop performing animations, for
example, the site might store that preference in `localStorage`
so that it can honor it in future visits. And by storing the preference, it generates an event that allows other windows displaying the same site to honor the request as well. As another
example, imagine a web-based image editing application that
allows the user to display tool palettes in separate windows.
When the user selects a tool, the application uses `localStor
age` to save the current state and to generate a notification to
other windows that a new tool has been selected.

Cookies

A *cookie* is a small amount of named data stored by the web
browser and associated with a particular web page or website.
Cookies were originally designed for server-side programming,
and at the lowest level, they are implemented as an extension
to the HTTP protocol. Cookie data is automatically transmitted between the web browser and web server, so server-side
scripts can read and write cookie values that are stored on the
client. This section demonstrates how client-side scripts can
also manipulate cookies using the `cookie` property of the Document object.

The API for manipulating cookies is an old one, which means
that it is universally supported. Unfortunately, the API is also
cryptic. There are no methods involved: cookies are queried,
set, and deleted by reading and writing the `cookie` property of
the Document object using specially formatted strings. The
lifetime and scope of each cookie can be individually specified

with cookie attributes. These attributes are also specified with specially formatted strings set on the same `cookie` property.

The subsections that follow explain the cookie attributes that specify lifetime and scope, and then demonstrate how to set and query cookie values in JavaScript.

Cookie Attributes: Lifetime and Scope

In addition to a name and a value, each cookie has optional attributes that control its lifetime and scope. Cookies are transient by default; the values they store last for the duration of the web browser session but are lost when the user exits the browser. Note that this is a subtly different lifetime than `sessionStorage`: cookies are not scoped to a single window, and their default lifetime is the same as the entire browser process, not the lifetime of any one window. If you want a cookie to last beyond a single browsing session, you must tell the browser how long (in seconds) you would like it to retain the cookie by specifying a *max-age* attribute. If you specify a lifetime, the browser will store cookies in a file and delete them only once they expire.

Cookie visibility is scoped by document origin as `localStorage` and `sessionStorage` are, and also by document path. This scope is configurable through cookie attributes *path* and *domain*. By default, a cookie is associated with, and accessible to, the web page that created it and any other web pages in the same directory or any subdirectories of that directory. If the web page *http://www.example.com/catalog/index.html* creates a cookie, for example, that cookie is also visible to *http://www.example.com/catalog/order.html* and *http://www.example.com/catalog/widgets/index.html*, but it is not visible to *http://www.example.com/about.html*.

This default visibility behavior is often exactly what you want. Sometimes, though, you'll want to use cookie values throughout a website, regardless of which page creates the cookie. For instance, if the user enters his mailing address in a form on one page, you may want to save that address to use as the default the next time he returns to the page and also as the default in an entirely unrelated form on another page where he is asked to enter a billing address. To allow this usage, you specify a *path* for the cookie. Then, any web page from the same web server whose URL begins with the path prefix you specified can share the cookie. For example, if a cookie set by *http://www .example.com/catalog/widgets/index.html* has its path set to "/catalog," that cookie is also visible to *http://www.example .com/catalog/order.html*. Or, if the path is set to "/," the cookie is visible to any page on the *http://www.example.com* web server.

Setting the *path* of a cookie to "/" gives scoping like that of `localStorage` and also specifies that the browser must transmit the cookie name and value to the server whenever it requests any web page on the site.

By default, cookies are scoped by document origin. Large websites may want cookies to be shared across subdomains, however. For example, the server at *order.example.com* may need to read cookie values set from *catalog.example.com*. This is where the *domain* attribute comes in. If a cookie created by a page on *catalog.example.com* sets its *path* attribute to "/" and its *domain* attribute to ".example.com," that cookie is available to all web pages on *catalog.example.com*, *orders.example.com*, and any other server in the *example.com* domain. If the *domain* attribute is not set for a cookie, the default is the hostname of the web server that serves the page. Note that you cannot set the domain of a cookie to a domain other than the domain of your server.

The final cookie attribute is a boolean attribute named *secure* that specifies how cookie values are transmitted over the network. By default, cookies are insecure, which means that they are transmitted over a normal, insecure HTTP connection. If a cookie is marked secure, however, it is transmitted only when the browser and server are connected via HTTPS or another secure protocol.

Setting Cookies

To associate a transient cookie value with the current document, simply set the **cookie** property to a string of the form:

```
name=value
```

For example:

```
var v = encodeURIComponent(document.lastModified);
document.cookie = "version=" + v;
```

The next time you read the **cookie** property, the name/value pair you stored is included in the list of cookies for the document. Cookie values cannot include semicolons, commas, or whitespace. For this reason, you may want to use the core JavaScript global function **encodeURIComponent()** to encode the value before storing it in the cookie.

A cookie written with a simple name/value pair lasts for the current web-browsing session but is lost when the user exits the browser. To create a cookie that can last across browser sessions, specify its lifetime (in seconds) with a **max-age** attribute. You can do this by setting the **cookie** property to a string of the form:

```
name=value; max-age=seconds
```

The following function sets a cookie with an optional max-age attribute:

```
// Store the name/value pair as a cookie, encoding
// the value with encodeURIComponent() in order to
// escape semicolons, commas, and spaces.
// If daysToLive is a number, set the max-age attribute
// so that the cookie expires after the specified
// number of days. Pass 0 to delete a cookie.
function setCookie(name, value, daysToLive) {
    var cookie = name + "=" + encodeURIComponent(value);
    if (typeof daysToLive === "number")
        cookie += "; max-age=" + (daysToLive*60*60*24);
    document.cookie = cookie;
}
```

Similarly, you can set the path, domain, and secure attributes of a cookie by appending strings of the following format to the cookie value before that value is written to the cookie property:

```
; path=path
; domain=domain
; secure
```

To change the value of a cookie, set its value again using the same name, path, and domain along with the new value. You can change the lifetime of a cookie when you change its value by specifying a new max-age attribute.

To delete a cookie, set it again using the same name, path, and domain, specifying an arbitrary (or empty) value, and a max-age attribute of 0.

Reading Cookies

When you use the cookie property in a JavaScript expression, the value it returns is a string that contains all the cookies that apply to the current document. The string is a list of *name = value* pairs separated from each other by a semicolon and a space. The cookie *value* does not include any of the attributes that may have been set for the cookie. In order to make use of the document.cookie property, you must typically call the split() method to break it into individual name-value pairs.

Once you have extracted the value of a cookie from the cookie property, you must interpret that value based on whatever format or encoding was used by the cookie's creator. You might, for example, pass the cookie value to decodeURICompo nent() and then to JSON.parse().

Example 14-1 defines a getCookie() function that parses the document.cookie property and returns an object whose properties specify the name and values of the document's cookies.

Example 14-1. Parsing the document.cookies property

```
// Return the document's cookies as an object of
// name/value pairs. Assume that cookie values
// are encoded with encodeURIComponent().
```

```
function getCookies() {
    var cookies = {}; // The object we return
    var all = document.cookie; // All cookies
    if (all === "") // If empty
        return cookies; // return an empty object
    // Split string into name=value pairs
    var list = all.split("; ");
    // Loop through the name=value pairs
    for(var i = 0; i < list.length; i++) {
        var cookie = list[i];
        // Split each pair at the = sign
        var p = cookie.indexOf("=");
        var name = cookie.substring(0,p);
        var value = cookie.substring(p+1);
        // Store the name and decoded value
        cookies[name] = decodeURIComponent(value);
    }
    return cookies;
}
```

Cookie Limitations

Cookies are intended for storage of small amounts of data by
server-side scripts, and that data is transferred to the server
each time a relevant URL is requested. The standard that defines cookies encourages browser manufacturers to allow un-
limited numbers of cookies of unrestricted size but does not
require browsers to retain more than 300 cookies total, 20
cookies per web server, or 4 KB of data per cookie (both name
and value count toward this 4 KB limit). In practice, browsers
allow many more than 300 cookies total, but the 4 KB size limit
may still be enforced by some.

Index

Symbols

! invert boolean value, 29, 41
! unary negation operator, 18
!= loose inequality/not equal operator, 13, 29, 38
!== strict inequality operator, 29, 37, 82
" " (string), 9
#top identifier, 168
$ identifier, 2
$ match end, 157
% modulo operator, 7, 32
& bitwise AND operator, 29, 35
&& logical AND, 30, 39
&= operator, 43
' ' (string), 9
(?!) negative lookahead assertion, 157
(?:) grouping only, 155
(?=) positive lookahead assertion, 157
* multiplication operator, 7, 29, 32
* repetition character, 153
* wildcard argument, 185
*= operator, 43
+ addition operator, 7, 32

+ concatenate strings, 29
+ convert to number, 29
+ repetition character, 153
+ unary plus operator, 18, 33
++ increment operator, 29, 33, 51
++ pre-/post-increment, 29
+= operator, 42, 193
, discard 1st operand, return 2nd, 30, 46
- negate number, 29
- subtraction operator, 7, 33
- unary minus operator, 33
-- decrement operator, 29, 34, 51
-- pre-/post-decrement, 29
. dot operator, 14
. value of property, 79
/ division operator, 7, 32
/* */ multi-line comment, 1
// single-line comment, 1
/[ ]/ regular expressions, 152
; empty statement, 52
; semicolon, 3
< less than operator, 29, 38
<= less than or equal operator, 29, 38

We'd like to hear your suggestions for improving our indexes. Send email to *index@oreilly.com*.

---

with statements, 51, 70, 220
writable attribute, 87

X

Z

About the Author

David Flanagan is a JavaScript programmer at Mozilla. His books with O'Reilly include *JavaScript: The Definitive Guide*, *jQuery Pocket Reference*, *The Ruby Programming Language*, and *Java in a Nutshell*. David has a degree in computer science and engineering from the Massachusetts Institute of Technology. He lives with his wife and children in the U.S. Pacific Northwest between the cities of Seattle, Washington, and Vancouver, British Columbia. David has a blog at *http://www.davidflanagan.com/*.

Colophon

The animal on the cover of *JavaScript Pocket Reference* is a Javan rhinoceros. All five species of rhinoceros are distinguished by their large size, thick armor-like skin, three-toed feet, and single or double snout horn. The Javan rhinoceros, along with the Sumatran rhinoceros, is a forest-dwelling species. The Javan rhinoceros is similar in appearance to the Indian rhinoceros, but it is smaller and has certain distinguishing characteristics (primarily skin texture).

The cover image is from the Dover Pictorial Archive. The cover font is Adobe ITC Garamond. The text font is Linotype Birka; the heading font is Adobe Myriad Condensed; and the code font is LucasFont's TheSansMonoCondensed.

Get even more for your money.

Join the O'Reilly Community, and register the O'Reilly books you own. It's free, and you'll get:

- $4.99 ebook upgrade offer
- 40% upgrade offer on O'Reilly print books
- Membership discounts on books and events
- Free lifetime updates to ebooks and videos
- Multiple ebook formats, DRM FREE
- Participation in the O'Reilly community
- Newsletters
- Account management
- 100% Satisfaction Guarantee

Registering your books is easy:
1. Go to: oreilly.com/go/register
2. Create an O'Reilly login.
3. Provide your address.
4. Register your books.

Note: English-language books only

To order books online:
oreilly.com/store

For questions about products or an order:
orders@oreilly.com

To sign up to get topic-specific email announcements and/or news about upcoming books, conferences, special offers, and new technologies:
elists@oreilly.com

For technical questions about book content:
booktech@oreilly.com

To submit new book proposals to our editors:
proposals@oreilly.com

O'Reilly books are available in multiple DRM-free ebook formats. For more information:
oreilly.com/ebooks

O'REILLY®

Spreading the knowledge of innovators   oreilly.com

The information you need, when and where you need it.

With Safari Books Online, you can:

Access the contents of thousands of technology and business books

- Quickly search over 7000 books and certification guides
- Download whole books or chapters in PDF format, at no extra cost, to print or read on the go
- Copy and paste code
- Save up to 35% on O'Reilly print books
- **New!** Access mobile-friendly books directly from cell phones and mobile devices

Stay up-to-date on emerging topics before the books are published

- Get on-demand access to evolving manuscripts.
- Interact directly with authors of upcoming books

Explore thousands of hours of video on technology and design topics

- Learn from expert video tutorials
- Watch and replay recorded conference sessions

O'REILLY®